Instructor's Manual

Intermediate MACRO

FIRST EDITION

Robert J. Barro

Prepared by

Dale Matcheck
Northwood University

Australia • Brazil • Japan • Korea • Mexico • Singapore • Spain • United Kingdom • United States

ISBN-13: 978-1-439-07963-8
ISBN-10: 1-439-07963-3

South-Western, Cengage Learning
2640 Eagan Woods Drive
Suite 220
Eagan, MN 55121

Cengage Learning is a leading provider of customized learning solutions with office locations around the globe, including Singapore, the United Kingdom, Australia, Mexico, Brazil, and Japan. Locate your local office at: **www.cengage.com/global**

Cengage Learning products are represented in Canada by Nelson Education, Ltd.

For your course and learning solutions, visit **www.cengage.com**

Purchase any of our products at your local college store or at our preferred online store **www.ichapters.com**

Printed in the United States of America
1 2 3 4 5 13 12 11 10 09

ED286

TABLE OF CONTENTS

Chapter 1: Thinking About Macroeconomics

Chapter Summary:

The chapter provides an overview of the important themes of the textbook. It provides a brief description of the important **economic aggregates** in the context of U.S. economic performance. Historical data on U.S. GDP, business cycles, inflation, and unemployment are examined.

After inspecting the available data, the process for developing theories to explain the data is described. The importance of modeling aggregate behavior on the basis of strong microeconomic foundations is emphasized. The supply and demand framework for analyzing markets is presented for the coffee market. Students who are rusty on their economic principles will appreciate this section. In this class, market clearing models of the macroeconomy provide the basic framework and other theories, such as the new Keynesian, are presented using the same basic tools.

Chapter Outline:

I. Output, Employment, and Prices in U.S. History

II. Economic Models

- A. Supply and Demand Analysis
- B. Flexible Versus Sticky Prices

Teaching Tips:

1. The chapter is motivational, so begin by telling students by discussing expectations. What can they expect from you? What can they expect from the book? What do you expect of them? Why study macro?

a. Use a concrete example to show that understanding the macroeconomic environment is as important to business managers and investors as understanding the weather is to sailors. A good recent example of this is the downturn in the U.S. housing market during the winter of 2006-2007 that pushed many sub-prime borrowers into default.

b. Economic thinking is systemic thinking- changes in one variable have repercussions throughout the system. In the previous example, consider how

This affected not only borrowers, but lenders, and possibly the entire economy. Could a better awareness of economic cycles with their booms and busts, along with more attention to current economic indicators have helped avoid those problems? From a policy perspective, do the monetary authorities have the means or the responsibility to limit the amount or the type of credit available in the economy?

2. When it comes to supply and demand analysis, some students may be out of practice. Consider augmenting the coffee market example with diagrams of real world market developments using articles from the Wall Street Journal.

Chapter 2: National-Income Accounting: Gross Domestic Product and the Price Level

Chapter Summary:

The chapter introduces the system of **National Income Accounts** with particular attention paid to the concept of GDP. The 3 conceptual approaches to GDP measurement (**production, expenditure, and income**) are described. Since goods produced are ultimately purchased, providing income to the seller, the 3 methods should yield similar results. The 4 categories of expenditure (**consumption, investment, government, and net exports**) are described in some detail; important attention to these descriptions now will help to avoid confusion later on. The assumption of a **closed economy** is discussed here and will be used consistently throughout the next 14 chapters. The difference between **nominal** and **real** values is discussed along with a description of the implicit price deflator. Differences between various price indices are discussed and a detailed look at the consumer price index (**CPI**) is featured in the "Back to Reality" section on page 31.

Chapter Outline:

I. Nominal and Real GDP
   A. Calculation of Real GDP
   B. Real GDP as a measure of Welfare

II. Alternative Views of GDP
   A. Expenditure Approach
   B. Income Approach
   C. Production Approach
   D. Seasonal Adjustment

III. Prices

Teaching Tips:

1. The National Bureau of Economic Research is a wonderful resource for teachers with internet access in the classroom. Up to the minute reports on a wide variety of leading indicators can help students obtain an up to the minute understanding of the economic conditions: available at http//nber.org/releases

2. Be sure to help students understand what GDP really measures by providing clear examples of what is *not* included: transfer payments, environmental damages, non-market production, and so on. It is important also to emphasize that it is not a measure of wealth because it is a *flow* variable, not a stock variable.

3. It is important for students to understand the strengths and weaknesses of using real GDP as indicator of economic welfare. Consider using the example of increased spending in the aftermath of the 9/11 attacks to discuss whether or not GDP adequately captures changes in social welfare.

4. The "Back to Reality" sections are an important feature of the textbook, providing students with examples of "real world" applications of economic theory. Students should be encouraged to read and discuss the "Problems with the consumer price index" on page 31.

5. Students should be encouraged to use price indices to make valid comparisons for data series other than GDP. For example, having students compare the evolution of the nominal federal minimum wage is an eye-opener. Have them compare the real salaries of minimum wage workers in San Diego, California and Hattiesburg Mississippi using regional price indices available at http://www.bestplaces.net. The regional CPI for San Diego is 177.1; for Hattiesburg it is 82.6. You can also use this site to discuss the limits of real GDP as a measure of living standards. If salaries could be adjusted for the difference in the cost of living, would students be indifferent between those two locations?

Answers to review questions, pg. 32

1. Nominal GDP is the market value of final goods and services produced within a nation's borders during the period, measured in current prices. Real GDP is nominal GDP measured in base year prices, also known as "GDP in constant dollars."

2. The implicit price deflator is a price index which is based on the weighted average price of all final goods and services produced; in the base year it is established at 100. The implicit price deflator is expressed as the ratio between nominal and real GDPx100. It differs from the CPI, which is a price index of a basket of consumer goods. Because of differences in the weights assigned to

various goods (they are fixed for longer periods), the CPI tends to show a higher rate of inflation than the implicit price deflator.

3. The 3 approaches to measuring GDP discussed in the chapter yield the same results because they are looking at the same transaction from different perspectives. The expenditure approach looks at the various types of spending on final goods and services. But that spending generates income for others, so the amount of spending should be equal to the amount of income (after adjusting for depreciation, net factor income earned abroad). The production approach measures the value of goods produced and sold by sector. Ultimately everything produced is sold and generates income for the factors of production, so there should be no difference in the estimates generated by the 3 approaches.

Answers to Problems for discussion, pg. 33

4. Official estimates of GDP do not measure welfare exactly, although higher GDP is highly correlated with widely accepted measures of welfare such as literacy, life expectancy, infant mortality rates and so forth. One of the reasons why GDP may underestimate the true change in welfare is because it fails to take into account non-market goods such as leisure. It also may fail to take into account changes in the quality of goods because these are not accurately captured in the implicit price deflator. On the other hand, GDP may overestimate changes welfare because it fails to take into the environmental impact of production. Clear cutting an old growth forest may simply convert a valuable non-market good to a less valuable market good, but the activity would tend to raise GDP. One way to take these effects into account is to incorporate the implicit value of nonmarket goods like leisure and environmental goods into a broader measure of welfare.

5. As one of many possible examples, consider the following data for Ireland, 2005 (€ million):

Gross Domestic Product (GDP) at current market prices	161,163
plus Net factor income from the rest of the world	-25,248
Gross National Product (GNP) at current market prices	135,914
EU subsidies	2,237
EU taxes	-432
Gross National Income (GNI) at current market prices	137,719
less provision for depreciation	-16,896
less Non EU taxes	-21,494

plus Non EU subsidies	925
Net National Product	100,254
Gross National Disposable Income (GNDI)	136,515

Source: Central Statistics Office of Ireland

The reconciliation used here is similar, but does not exactly correspond to the example used in the text book. One interesting observation here is that Ireland has a significant difference between GDP and GNP, due perhaps to a large influx of foreigners participating in the "Celtic Tiger's" economic boom.

Chapter 3: Economic Growth

Chapter Summary:

The chapter discusses the importance of economic growth for raising living standards over time and provides a basic framework for understanding the sources of economic growth. Statistics are provided which allow for international comparisons of growth rates and GDP; the patterns emerging from the data are discussed. The neoclassical theory of growth is described using the **Solow model**. Beginning with **the production function** that exhibits **diminishing returns** to each input and **constant returns to scale**, the **steady state** level of income, is described, as are the basic components of **growth accounting**. These concepts are essential both for understanding and motivating the more complex material found in the next two chapters.

Outline:

I. The Importance of Economic Growth

II. Facts About Economic Growth
- A. World Economic Growth, 1960-2000
- B. World Poverty and Income Inequality
- C. Long Term Growth in the U.S. and Other Wealthy Countries
- D. Patterns of World Economic Growth

III. Theory of Economic Growth
- A. The Production Function
- B. Growth Accounting
- C. The Solow Growth Model
  1. Growth Rate of the Capital Stock
  2. Growth Rate of Labor
  3. Growth Rate of Capital and Output Per Worker
  4. The Transition and the Steady State

Teaching Tips:

1. -"The Rule of 70" is a rough method of demonstrating how small changes in the economic growth rate lead to large changes in living standards over time. The approximate number of years it takes for income to double is given by the ratio 70/r, where r is the growth rate. Since 70 is a good number to use for an average lifetime, the growth rate is an estimate of the number of times income

will double during a person's lifetime. Ask them to make a hypothetical comparison of a few countries that begin with $5,000 in current GDP per person but grow at rates of 1%, 2%, 3% and 4% annually. After 70 years, the approximate income in each country will be $10,000, $20,000, $40,000, and $80,000. Have them graph the income level against the growth rate to show the nonlinear effects of compounding.

2. As a way of motivating the material, have the students "guess" the purchasing power in the major regions of the world. Then have them check their answers against the data found in the chapter. Did they accurately rank the regions? Did they come close to the actual purchasing power?

3. The material in this chapter introduces some algebraic symbols with which economists are very familiar. However, students will have trouble keeping track of what all these letters stand for. If you can reserve a space on the board with a key to the symbols used (K=capital, Y= Income, etc.) your students will be able to keep up. You may also copy the key provided on page x of this manual, which includes all the symbols used in the text in the order in which they are introduced.

4. After discussing the equations introduced in the text using algebraic symbols, instructors might consider using numerical examples to have the students graph a simple production function. Numerical examples are less abstract and therefore easier for many students to relate to.

5. Much of the excitement and controversy in macroeconomics comes from the way in which the economy is modeled, but students are less likely to be enthusiastic by the intricacies of model building. So the temptation for the instructor is to gloss over the modeling process or simplify it to the extent that it loses its intrinsic interest. This temptation to "dumb down" the presentation must be avoided if the student is to grasp the process of discovery and argument used by practicing economists. At the same time, the possibility of confusion and boredom is very real. That is why the "back to reality" boxes provide in the text are valuable. Each instructor should incorporate a discussion of these examples into their lecture, and seek to develop additional "back to reality" examples as much as possible.

6. Remind students of the law of diminishing returns to capital. Ask them what would happen to their test scores if they had to share their textbook with a friend on the night before an exam. What about sharing with 3, 10, or 20?

Answers to Review questions, pg. 62

1. A production function associates a particular level of output with each possible combination of inputs and technology. Growth of output is proportional to changes in the level of technology, but because of diminishing returns, output grows less than proportionately to changes in each input.

2. Marginal product of capital is the additional output obtained from an additional unit of capital employed. Average Product of Capital is the total output divided by the total amount of capital employed. Since the average product includes the effects of all the previous units of capital employed, it may differ considerably from the marginal product. Although it is theoretically possible for the average product to be less than the average product, that is ruled out in our model by the assumption that diminishing returns to capital sets in immediately- every unit of capital employed contributes less than all that came before it, so the marginal product is always less than the average.

3. In our model we assumed that the labor force was growing ($n>0$). In this case a positive savings rate is necessary, but not sufficient to raise the level of capital per worker. The savings rate must be sufficiently large to replace worn out capital, and add additional capital to keep up with the rate of growth in the labor force, as summarized in equation (3.16) Applying a little algebra to equation (3.16) shows that for $\Delta k/k$ to be positive, $s(y/k)-s\delta-n>0$, or that $s > n/((y/k)-\delta)$ if $(y/k)-\delta)$ is positive. (If $(y/k)-\delta)$ were negative, then capital stock would shrink regardless of the saving rate).

4. A positive saving rate cannot guarantee growth in the long run, due to diminishing returns. The average product of capital would continue to fall and the amount of depreciation would increase as the capital stock grew larger. Eventually, the capital stock would reach a point where all the savings would be needed simply to replace the depreciated capital stock and keep up with the growth in the labor force, nothing left over to increase the capital per worker. At that point the economy will have reached the "steady state."

Answers to Problems for discussion, pg. 63

6. Constant returns to scale implies that for our production function Y=A*F(K,L) has the property that xY=A*F(xK,xL) for any constant x.

Now if we choose x=1/L, then Y/L=A*F(K/L,L/L) = A*F(K/L,1)=A*f(k), where F(K/L,1) defines a new function in the variable K/L=k. We denote the new function F(K/L,1)= f(k), so that A*F(K/L,1)=A*f(k).

7. a. A=the state of technology, K is the capital stock, and L is the labor force.

b. A is a scalar factor, so that when A increases by "x percent", Y will increase by "x percent."

c. A marginal product that is always positive implies that each additional unit of input will increase output by some positive amount.

d. It means that each additional unit of input is associated with a smaller increase in output than the previous unit. $MPK=\alpha(K^{\alpha}L^{1-\alpha})/K$. Since α is less than 1, an increase in the value of K will cause the denominator to increase faster than the numerator in this equation, and the MPK will diminish as K increases.

e. Yes. Constant returns to scale implies that if we multiply each input by a particular factor, output will increase by the same factor. If we multiply the inputs by a factor of x, we get:

$$A(xK)^{\alpha}(xL)^{1-\alpha}$$
$$=Ax^{\alpha}x^{1-\alpha}K^{\alpha}L^{1-\alpha}$$
$$=xA\,K^{\alpha}L^{1-\alpha}$$
$$=xY$$

8.

Increase in variable:	Effect on k*:
a. Saving rate (s)	increase
b. Technology (A)	increase
c. depreciation rate (δ)	decrease
d. pop. growth rate (n)	decrease

9. a. In the steady state, $sy/k-s\delta-n=0$ and $y/k=Ak^{\alpha}/k = Ak^{\alpha-1}$. Combining these two expressions yields $sAk^{\alpha-1}=s\delta+n$; or $k^{\alpha-1}=(s\delta+n)/sA$. Raising each side by the exponent $1/(\alpha-1)$ yields: $k^*=[(s\delta+n)/sA]^{1/(\alpha-1)}$. Substituting this into the production function yields $y^*=k^{*\alpha}=[(s\delta+n)/sA]^{\alpha/(\alpha-1)}$.

   b. $c^*=(1-s)(y^*-\delta k^*)$ Since savings in the steady state is just sufficient to replace capital, we have $s(y^*-\delta k^*)=nk^*$, so that $c^*= y^*-\delta k^*-nk^*$.

   c. $\Delta k/k= sy/k-s\delta-n= sAk^{\alpha-1}-s\delta-n$ or $sA/k^{1-\alpha}-s\delta-n$. Since k appears in the denominator of the first term, larger values of k imply smaller growth rates. Because of diminishing returns, y must grow more slowly as you near the steady state, first because of diminishing returns to k and also because k grows more slowly.

10. a. Using the results from problem number 9 above, but substituting $\alpha=1$, we get $\Delta k/k= sA-s\delta-n$; k grows at a constant rate. The s(y/k) curve is a horizontal line with vertical intercept at sA.

   b. $\Delta k/k= sA-s\delta-n$; Since $y=Ak$, $\Delta y=A\Delta k$ and $\Delta y/y=A\Delta k/Ak$ or $\Delta k/k$. Output per worker will also grow at a constant rate (equal to the growth rate in capital).

   c. There is no diminishing returns to capital in this case. There are several possible plausible explanations for this assumption; one is that there is "learning by doing", so that as the economy industrializes knowledge multiplies rapidly and augments capital. Perhaps social institutions also develop along with capital (for example, the development of legal corporations and contract law). Even with this broader understanding of the process of capital accumulation, it would seem as though diminishing returns to capital would set in at some point.

Chapter 4: Working With The Solow Growth Model

Chapter Summary:

Chapter 3 introduced the basic neoclassical model of economic growth and its major results: growth rates tend to diminish over time as the economy approaches a steady state level of output per worker. Now the parameters of the model are manipulated to show how changes in the key parameters affect growth rates and the steady state level of income. Using the key equation describing the accumulation of capital, changes in savings rates, population growth rates or the labor force, and technology are analyzed. The steady state level of output per worker is shown to increase as savings rates or technology increase. The steady state level of output per worker falls as the population or grows. Changes to the labor force can affect the growth rate because they change the capital labor ratio, but they do not affect the ultimate steady state level of output per worker. In all of these cases, the curves in the basic steady state diagram are shifted to illustrate the effects of changing parameter values on the steady state level of capital.

The concept of **absolute convergence** is examined next. Since the rate of capital accumulation per worker is essentially determined by the current stock of capital per worker, lesser developed countries are predicted by the model to grow more quickly than developed countries. However, the capital per worker will only generate faster growth rates if the values of the other parameters (savings, technology, population growth, etc.) are somewhat comparable. This implies that there is only **conditional convergence**. The empirical evidence presented in the chapter confirms this view. Data from more than 100 countries suggest that conditional convergence exists, but there is little evidence to confirm the existence of absolute convergence.

Outline:

I. Working With The Solow Model

    A. A Change in the Savings Rate
    B. A Change in the Technology Level
    C. Changes in Labor Input
    D. Changes in the Population Growth Rate

II. Convergence

    A. Absolute Convergence

B. Facts About Convergence

C. Conditional Convergence

III. Appendix: The Speed of Convergence

Teaching Tips:

1. If the students are familiar by this point with the equation for growth in the capital stock (equation 3.16) and the diagram which illustrates it, the diagrams provide clear predictions for the effects of changing parameter values. Each diagram should be accompanied by an intuitive explanation for the result as well.

2. In many countries in Europe, birthrates have fallen below the replacement rate, as seen in the data below. The Solow model suggests that this should generate increasing productivity and a higher steady state level of income. However, the low birthrates have instead caused public concern and even government intervention (in the form of tax benefits for larger families and subsidized child care for working mothers). Clearly there is more to the population story than the simple Solow model indicates. The problem here is that the labor force participation rate is not constant. As the population ages, the labor force participation rate decreases. This puts their generous social pension and health care systems at risk. Also, though a falling labor force may increase the average product of labor, the total product of labor will clearly fall, and the average living standard of retirees along with it.

Here are some statistics for European fertility rates (2.1 children per woman is the replacement rate):

Ireland: 1.99
France: 1.90
Norway: 1.81
Sweden 1.75
UK: 1.74
Netherlands: 1.73
Germany: 1.37
Italy: 1.33
Spain: 1.32
Greece: 1.29
Source: Eurostat - 2004 figures

3. The section on Malthus (Extending the Model, pg. 79) provides fascinating reading, but it would be a mistake to understand it as a historical argument long since discarded. The ideas of Malthus have had a revival as the environmental movement has grown over the last few decades. Although land may no longer be a limiting factor, the attention has now shifted to such things as climate change and fossil fuel consumption. A relatively recent example of this is Jared Diamond's book, "collapse".

4. Is it right to consider people just another mouth to feed? The late economist Julian Simon made the opposite point- that individual creativity is "the ultimate resource." Every mind produces new ideas that make every other minds more productive. How would this idea change the way we think about "n" in our model?

5. The Solow model presented here is used to conduct positive economic analysis – this causes that. But there are important public policy issues associated with the theory. If the theory is accurate, should the government take design policies to influence parameter values? The one-child policy in China is one example, a sales tax to discourage consumption and encourage savings is another.

Answers to Review Questions (pg. 90):

1: Recall that the saving curve in figure 4.4 depends on the average product of capital per worker: y/k, and that y depends only on output per worker, not the absolute level of labor or capital (see equation 3.2 on page 49). Therefore, the level of saving depends only on the capital labor ratio; changes in the absolute levels of K or L do not shift the curve. Constant returns to scale is a key assumption here because it was used to derive equation 3.2. Given Y=A*F(K,L) and constant returns to scale, multiplying Y by 1/L yields: Y/L=A*F(K/L,L/L) or y=A*f(k). If constant returns to scale were not found, the output per worker would depend on the absolute sizes of K and L, and not merely the ratio between them.

2. An increase in n will increase the rate at which capital per worker is depleted over time. This is illustrated on the graph by an upward shift in the horizontal line (as in figure 4.6.) For any given savings rate, this will result in a lower steady state level of capital and output per worker. However, the absolute level

of output will continue to increase. An economy with a faster rate of population growth will grow more quickly after reaching its steady state.

3. Convergence, as used in the theory of economic growth, refers to the tendency of less developed economies to grow more quickly than more mature economies. The theory is based on the idea that the growth rate will slow as an economy approaches the steady state level of capital per worker. Absolute convergence predicts that poor countries will grow more quickly regardless of their eventual steady state level of output. Conditional convergence predicts this pattern only if the countries have similar steady state levels of output. This would require, among other things, that the countries have similar technology, savings rates, and population growth rates.

4. The Solow model does not predict that all countries must reach the same steady state. If it did, then the results in figure. 4.9 would be problematic. As it is, the model includes various determinants of the steady state level of output which may vary from country to country. The theory of conditional convergence suggests that relatively poor countries will tend to "catch up" over time to countries with similar savings rates, population growth, and technology.

Answers to Problems for Discussion (pg. 90)

5. a. Yes, the growth rate in capital at any given period will depend on the savings rate in that period. However, the idea that the economy approaches a steady state level of per-capita income cannot be assumed.

   b. A pattern of rising savings rates would offset to some extent the effects of diminishing returns and depreciation on capital accumulation. The increase in the savings rate could cause the growth rate to increase over time. This would reduce the tendency toward convergence.

   c. A tendency for savings rates to fall at higher levels of income would reinforce the effects of diminishing returns and capital depreciation on capital accumulation; this would increase the tendency toward convergence.

   d. A small increase in the level of consumption in the present when someone is poor is likely to provide a higher rate of marginal utility than a similar increase when they are rich, due to diminishing marginal utility of consumption. Therefore, it may seem more likely that a poor person would save less than a wealthy person with similar preferences. This is the basis for the well known prediction that the marginal propensity to consume falls as income rises. However, this is complicated by the fact that the rate of return on savings should be higher when capital is relatively scarce; this would provide a relatively strong incentive to invest in capital poor countries. So for example, we observe that savings rates in China, which is still a relatively less developed country, are much higher than in the U.S.

6. a. It is valid for each period, however, the idea that the economy approaches a steady state level of per-capita income cannot be assumed.

   b. A pattern of falling population growth would offset to some extent the effects of diminishing returns and depreciation on capital accumulation. The increase in the rate of capital accumulation could cause the growth rate of output per person to increase over time. This would reduce the tendency toward convergence.

   c. A tendency for population growth rates to increase would have the opposite effect demonstrated in part b above. The rising population growth would reinforce the effects of diminishing returns and capital depreciation on capital per worker; this would increase the tendency toward convergence.

   d. Malthus predicted that population growth rates would increase as a function of income per worker, because it was excess population in his model which caused population growth to cease; in his view, it was mortality rates associated with poverty. That poverty was the result of diminishing returns to agricultural land, which could not be accumulated after a certain point. However, in the steady state conceived by Malthus, income per capita reaches its lowest possible point, and it is not depreciation of capital, but a decrease in the population growth that enables people to maintain even that miserable level of income. However much Malthus's model might have made sense at one point in human history, it is totally contradicted by the modern world. Today, the major resource is capital rather than land, and we observe that population growth rates decline as per capita income rises. This is primarily due to the fact that birth rates seem to be inversely related to per-capita income. Therefore, case b seems more plausible in a modern industrial economy.

Chapter 5: Conditional Convergence and Long-Run Economic Growth

Chapter Summary:

The previous chapters introduced a model of growth which was based on the accumulation of capital per worker (capital deepening). The assumption of diminishing marginal returns led to the conclusion that there was an ultimate limit to growth in income per worker: the so called "steady state". In this chapter, alternative models are discussed which allow for continuous growth.

One factor that allows for this possibility is a broader interpretation of capital to include human and infrastructure capital. The marginal returns to investment in human and infrastructure capital augment the returns to physical capital. While the production function may be subject to diminishing marginal returns in any of these three types of capital, investment in all three types leads to constant returns – the so called "Ak model". In this case, the average product of capital need not diminish as the amount of capital per worker expands, and there is no reason for the rate of capital accumulation to decline over time… there is no "steady state". Capital and output per worker grow at a constant rate. One important conclusion of this model is that there is no convergence between rich and poor countries.

The second factor that might lead to continuous growth is technological progress. The Solow model assumes that technological progress is exogenous: that the technology parameter A grows at a constant rate. In this case the accumulation of capital per worker will not end; technological progress offsets the impact of diminishing returns on the average product of capital. Output per worker will grow at a constant rate; but one of the more interesting aspects of this model is that growth in output per worker will grow faster than the rate of technological progress. This is due to the additional capital accumulation induced by the higher level of output per worker.

Endogenous growth theories attempt to identify the sources of technological progress within the model. Most of these focus on investment in research and development as a major determinant of technological change. Given the potential positive externalities associated with technological discoveries, the private return to R&D spending may be substantially less than the social rate of return. Countries that develop institutions that increase the returns to private R&D spending should experience faster rates of technological progress. The Romer model is a prominent example of endogenous growth theory. In this case, the private return on investment in R&D is dependent on such things as the efficiency of the regulatory process, the size of the market for the innovation, or the security of intellectual property rights.

Another source of technological progress is technological diffusion; many examples exist of countries which did not innovate a technological change, but were able to adopt it. In particular, a technology gap between a less developed country and more advanced economies can be closed quickly in this way; East Asia is a prime example. Economists believe that this process was aided by the relative openness of these economies to trade, the relatively high levels of education, and the relatively well functioning legal systems that are found in this region.

Chapter Outline:

I. Conditional Convergence in Practice
   A. Recent Research on the Determinants of Economic Growth
   B. Examples of Conditional Convergence
II. Long Run Economic Growth
   A. Models with Constant Average Product of Capital
   B. Exogenous Technological Progress
      1. The Steady State Growth Rate
      2. Steady State Saving
      3. The Transition Path and Convergence
   C. Endogenous Growth Theory
      1. Technological Innovation
         a. Romer Model
      2. Technological Diffusion
III. Conclusion: What We Know About Economic Growth

Teaching Tips:

1. A good introduction to the themes of this chapter and a fine way to introduce students to a quality economics blog is to direct them to this entry: http://www.becker-posner-blog.com/archives/2005/04/will_china_beco.html . The article contains Nobel Prize winner Gary Becker's opinions on whether or not China will "catch up" with the U.S. and offers some interesting historical comparisons.

2. The "Back to Reality" discussion of pop star Bono's meeting with the author is sure to generate some heated discussion about the effectiveness about international aid for foreign development. If you decide to offer extra credit opportunities, consider having the students provide an update on the economic performance of countries that were targeted by "Jubilee 2000."

3. The concept of "human capital" and the way in which it is used to justify the Ak model requires careful explanation.

4. A side by side comparison of the assumptions, specifications, and results of the three models discussed in the chapter will help students appreciate the similarities and differences.

5. One of the strengths of the book is that it is allows students to see the way the process by which various assumptions in the modeling process lead to different theoretical results; and the data available concerning real world results can either support or cast doubt on a particular model. Students should be encouraged to think critically about the strengths and weaknesses of each model. How do the models differ, and how would these differences show up in the available data? What kinds of tests could help researchers distinguish between competing theories of economic growth?

6. In the Romer model, spending on R&D is used as a proxy for technology progress, and that there are no diminishing returns to technology. This implies that there are no diminishing returns to R&D spending?

Answers to review questions, pg. 117

1. The exogenous growth in technology would lead to positive growth rates in both output and output per worker. The growth would come from two sources: the technological improvement (A), and the increase in the capital per worker (k). The contribution of each of these factors to growth rate in output per worker is given by equation 5.8 in the text. The capital per worker grows because of additional savings made possible by the higher level of output.

2. Differences in the growth rates can be explained by differences in the factors that determine the steady state level of income in each region. As saw in chapter 4, differences in savings rates, population growth and technology can have significant effects on the steady state level of income. East Asian countries are typically found to have relatively private and public savings rates during the

period. If we allow the parameter "A" to represent not just technology but economic efficiency in general, then other factors can also be identified. In particular, economists have focused on the legal and political institutions (including corruption), the openness to trade, health and education, and the relative size of the public sector as potential determinants of economic efficiency. In most of these areas, the East Asian nations had an advantage over the nations of sub-Saharan Africa. The theory of conditional convergence predicts if countries start with the same level of capital per worker, countries with a relatively high steady state level of output per worker will grow more quickly than the others. The story of Africa and Asia seems to fit the theory.

Answers to Problems for discussion, pg. 117

3. a. The key to understanding Galton's fallacy is to recognize that some of the variation in height is due to chance. For the sake of clarity, let us take an example where height is entirely due to chance: the height of the father has no predictive power on the height of the son. In particular, suppose that the height of the child can take on one of three values: short, tall or average, and that the probability of each outcome is exactly 1/3, regardless of the father's height. In this case, short fathers will have children who are, on average, taller than themselves. Tall fathers will have on average, children who are shorter than themselves. This may give the appearance of "height convergence"; but in fact the distribution of heights will remain unchanged: 1/3 of the population will be short, 1/3 will be tall, and 1/3 will be average.

Applying the logic outlined above to the case of rich and poor countries, we find that the appearance of convergence is possible even though incomes are not becoming more equal. At any particular point in time, the distribution of income per person will be determined to a certain extent by "chance"- that is, by events and circumstances not described in our growth model. These can have positive negative effects. If, over time, the good and bad effects balance out, then we would expect that wealthier countries have experienced "good luck" in the past and poorer countries have experienced "bad luck" over the same period. Since there is no systematic probability for either kind of luck to persist from period to period, the likelihood is for rich countries to grow more slowly as their luck "regresses to the mean". Likewise, poor countries will grow more quickly as their luck "regresses to the mean". Poor countries can grow more quickly than rich countries without changing the dispersion of income.

b. In part "a" to this question, we recognized that part of the growth rate of income per person is due to chance. But obviously, the theory of growth we learned in the text suggests that much of it can be predicted by specific factors- in particular, by the difference between current capital-worker ratio and its steady state value. It is reasonable to expect that during the earlier period (1880-1970) that some regions in the U.S. were closer to their steady state than others. Thus, much of the convergence could be attributed to the differences in the capital per worker that existed at that time. As the various regions developed, these differences diminished, and the apparent convergence in more recent times is due to random variations in growth rates between the states.

c. Conditional convergence implies that rich and poor countries with different steady states will not converge, but their will be groups of countries for which convergence will be observed. . If technological change allows steady state growth, then each group would be expected to have a different steady state growth rate as seen in equation (5.12).
The next question is, why would the rate of technological change differ among groups of countries? The answer lies in the institutions that encourage innovation or adoption of new technology. Countries which are relatively open to trade have high education levels, and a well functioning legal and political system, including support for intellectual property rights.

Chapter 6: Markets, Prices, Supply, and Demand

Chapter Summary:

This is the first chapter of a new unit on the nature of economic fluctuations. Up to this point, the text has focused on the relatively steady increase of production over long periods of time based entirely on supply side factors. In this unit, the role of the demand side is developed, short term fluctuations in employment and output are analyzed. In every theory of the business cycle, a crucial role is attributed to the price system. When it functions well, it acts as a "shock absorber" in the economy, stabilizing output and employment, and when it functions poorly, it can amplify shocks throughout the economy.

In the chapter, the market process is modeled using the familiar supply and demand approach in 4 important markets: the market for goods, the market for labor services, the market for capital services, and the market for bonds. In each case the factors that determine the supply and demand are described and the market clearing conditions identified. The links between these markets are established by examining the motives and behavior of the household decision makers in their various roles as producers, lenders, suppliers and consumers. The distribution of income that occurs when all four markets clear is divided entirely between suppliers of capital and labor services, and is based on the marginal contribution of each to total output. Since a competitive equilibrium under these conditions eliminates uncertainty and risk, the opportunity for profit is eliminated, and the share of profits in the economy is zero.

Chapter Outline:

I. Introduction: Markets, Prices, Supply and Demand
II. Four Key Markets in the Macroeconomy
  A. The Goods Market
  B. The Labor Market
  C. The Rental Market
  D. The Bond Market
  E. Money as a Medium of Exchange
III. Household Income and Spending
  A. Sources of Income
  B. Household Expenditures

C. Household Budget Constraint

IV. Market Clearing for Labor and Capital Services
   A. Profit Motive and the Demand for Resources
   B. The Market for Labor Services
      1. Demand for Labor
      2. Supply of Labor
      3. Clearing of the Labor Market
         a. equilibrium real wage
   C. The Market for Capital Services
      1. Demand for Capital Services
      2. Supply of Capital Services
      3. Clearing of the Capital Market
         a. equilibrium interest rate
   D. Profit in Equilibrium

Teaching Tips:

1. As we have seen before, the introduction of so many new symbols is likely to lead to confusion among the students. Teachers should consider posting a symbol key prominently on the board. You may consider distributing copies of the symbol key found at the end of this chapter. As always, student understanding will increase with numerical examples and practice.

2. The discussion of the bond market provides an opportunity to introduce students to one of the truly useful economic indicators. The "markets lineup" section of the Wall Street Journal will have the latest yield curve and other information on bond markets. Discussion of the various assets and interest rates will provide the basis for discussion of risk premiums and other details mentioned in the text and in the end of chapter problems, especially problem #6.

3. Although students may be aware of the concept of zero economic profit as a condition for long run equilibrium, it is worth explaining the relation of zero economic profit and "normal accounting profit", which is perhaps better described as the rate of return on capital ownership. It may also be helpful to review the effects of economic profit on exit and entry.

Answers to review questions, pg. 147

1. Money and prices are a convenient unit of measurement, but they are not fixed units like feet or inches. Ignoring changes in the value of money would be similar to ignoring changes between kilometers and miles per hour when

establishing acceptable speed limits. In Canada, where speed is measured in kilometers, 100 is associated with a particular level of safety. A speed limit of 100 in the U.S., where speeds are measured in miles per hour, would generate a much lower level of safety. Similarly, an agreement to accept a wage of $100 dollars per day when the prices are low may provide a relatively comfortable standard of living, but at a high price level, the comfort associated with $100 wage would be substantially reduced. In the early years of the 20th century, $5 per day was considered more than adequate to maintain a middle class lifestyle… what kind of lifestyle would that wage support today? Clearly it is not the money itself, but the things that money can buy, that households care about. If the prices of all goods, services and assets were to double, the purchasing power and wealth of households would not be affected.

2. A change in a household's net asset position during the period is a flow variable, the accumulated effects of these changes is a stock variable. For example, a person who has $100 in assets at the beginning of the period and a negative savings of $10 during the period will still be left with $90 in assets by the end of the period. They have negative *saving* during this particular period, but because of past decisions, they still have positive *savings*.

3. The household budget constraint is given by equation (6.12)

$$C+(1/P)*\circledcirc B + \circledcirc K=\circledcirc/P +(w/P)*L + i*(B/P + K)$$

This shows that real consumption plus real saving= real household income.

The graph is of a line with real consumption (C) as the independent variable, and real saving ($(1/P)*\circledcirc B + \circledcirc K$) as the dependent variable. We can subtract C from both sides of equation (6.12) to obtain:

$$(1/P)*\circledcirc B + \circledcirc K=\circledcirc/P +(w/P)*L + i*(B/P + K)-C$$

Which is a linear equation of the form real savings =a+ bC, where a is the intercept and is equal to real household income ($\circledcirc/P +(w/P)*L + i*(B/P + K)$), and b is the slope and is equal to -1. The line shows that there is a one to one tradeoff between increases in consumption and reductions in saving.

4. An increase in the real wage rate, w/P reduces the quantity of labor demanded. This conclusion is based on the shape of the demand curve shown in figure 6.4. on page 139. The demand curve for labor represents the marginal

value of each worker to the firm, and is downward sloping because of the diminishing marginal returns assumption.

5. The answer to this question is analogous to question 4, as shown in figure 6.6 on page 142.

Answers to Problems for discussion, pg. 147

6a. The rate of interest on the bond will be given by the formula:

$$i = (\text{principal} - P^B) / P^B$$

A positive rate of interest requires that $(\text{principal} - P^B) > 0$ or $P^B < \$1000$. If not, the rate of return on the bond would be negative.

6b. Using the formula given in part (6a) we have $i = (\$1000 - P^B) / P^B$

6c. An increase in the purchase price reduces the rate of interest because it increases the size of the denominator while reducing the size of the numerator.

6d. \$1 invested for 2 years at an interest rate I would be worth $\$1(1+i)$ at the end of the first year and $\$1(1+i)(1+i) = \$1(1+i)^2$ at the end of the second year. We can use this formula to compute the annual interest rate implied by bond which sells for P^B today and generates a payoff of \$1000 two years from now:

$$P^B(1+i)^2 = \$1000 \quad \text{or} \quad (1+i)^2 = \$1000 / P^B$$

Taking the square root of both sides and then subtracting 1 from each side yields:

$$i = (\$1000 / P^B)^{1/2} - 1$$

7a. Purchasing the two year bond is equivalent to purchasing the one year bond and reinvesting the proceeds at maturity in another one year bond. So our investor has a choice of either investing in an asset that yields (per \$1 invested) $(1+i_t)(1+i_{t+1})$ or he can invest in the 2 year bond in which case he will earn $(1+i^2_t)(1+i^2_t)$ per dollar invested. (Remember the 2 in the superscript is to denote a 2 year bond; it is not an exponent.) It should be clear from a casual inspection that the rate on the 2 year bond should be approximately equal to the average of the 1 year bond rates. For example, if the one year rates are 10% this year and are expected to be12% next year, then the rate on the two year bond should be approximately 11%. If the two year rate were much higher than that, lenders would sell the one year bond and purchase the two year, which reduce the spread between them. If the two year rate were much lower than 11%, lenders would sell off the two year bond and purchase the one year bond, causing the spread to narrow once again.

7b. If short term rates are expected to rise as in the previous example, then the long term rate will by higher than the short term rate. This is because the long term rate must take into account next years short term rates in order to be attractive to today's lenders. This may explain why, in a growing economy, the yield curve is relatively steep; lenders expect the central bank to raise short term interest rates at some point to keep inflation in check. It may also explain why, in a weakening economy, the yield curve can "invert", since the weakness in the economy may cause lenders to expect the central bank to reduce short term rates in the near future in order to stimulate the economy. An inverted yield curve has historically been a fairly reliable leading indicator of an economic downturn.

7c. If future short term rates are not known with certainty, then the decision to hold long term bonds entails some risk. Unexpected movements in short term rates could leave long term bond holders with lower rates of return. This could cause prices of long term bonds to fall below the average of the expected short term rates, which would result in higher rates for long term bonds.

8a and b. The intermediary will not change the aggregate zero balance of lending. It takes $1 of lending to generate $1 of borrowing. However the intermediary will typically charge a higher rate on loans than they offer on deposits. This means that the interest income received by lenders will be less than the interest expenses of the borrower. The difference is the bank's compensation for coordinating the actions of borrowers and lenders.

8c. The intermediary has experience and information that borrowers and lenders lack. The ability to evaluate the creditworthiness of potential borrowers and arrange terms which fit the unique needs of both borrowers and lenders is relatively scarce. They also have a diversified portfolio of assets which pools the risk of default among all of its depositors. Thus, banks and other financial intermediaries can substantially reduce the risk and the transactions costs associated with borrowing and lending.

Handout: Symbols Used in Chapter 6

Symbol:	Concept:	Definition:
Y	Real Goods Produced	The quantity of goods and services produced during the period.
A	State of Technology	A technological "multiplier" that makes capital and labor services more productive.
K	Real Capital	Assets such as buildings, equipment, materials, employed in the production process.
L	Real Labor	The amount of labor services employed in the production process.
F(K,L)	Production Function	A function which relates the each possible combination of capital and labor input to a particular value of output.
X^s	quantity of "x" supplied	The superscript s refers to the supply side of the market for "X".
X^d	quantity of "x" demanded	The superscript "d" refers to the demand side of the market for "X".
M	The nominal quantity of money	The quantity of money circulating in the economy expressed in dollars
M/P	The real quantity of money	The quantity of money circulating in the economy expressed in terms of its real purchasing power
w	The nominal wage rate	The amount paid for one unit of labor services, expressed in dollars.
w/P	The real wage rate	The amount paid for one unit of labor services expressed in terms of its real purchasing power
R	The nominal rental rate for capital	The amount paid for one unit of capital services, expressed in dollars.
R/P	The real rental rate for capital	The amount paid for one unit of capital services, in terms of its real purchasing power
P	The Price Level	A price index which expresses the cost of a basket of all goods and services in the economy. It is the price paid for one unit of Y.
i	The nominal rate of interest	The rate of return on money loaned out (in our model, the rate of return on bonds) expressed as a percentage of the principal.
r	The real rate of interest	The rate of return on money loaned out (in our model, the rate of return on bonds) adjusted for inflation. r=i-inflation.
B	The nominal value of Bonds	The quantity of Bonds ("I owe yous") expressed in terms of dollars.
◎	Nominal Profit	Income from sales- wage and rental payments, expressed in dollars.
◎X	"Delta X" or "The change in X"	The difference between the current value of variable x and its previous value

Chapter 7: Consumption, Saving, and Investment

Chapter Summary:

The theory that explains the relative stability of consumption spending and the relative volatility of investment spending begins with the assumption that consumption is an **intertemporal choice**. The chapter describes an intertemporal consumption choice constrained by income from assets and labor, and with the assumption that credit markets are readily available to borrow against future income or lend current income. In this environment, **consumption smoothing** is the primary result: changes in **permanent income** will generate a marginal propensity to consume near 1; temporary changes in income will generate only modest changes in consumption. The savings (or dissaving) that results from these temporary changes will affect investment in capital during the period.

The consumer's decision is presented first using a 2 period model which can be used to make the general points, later the household budget constraint is extended to many periods. A key point here is that future income is not equivalent to current income, but must be converted to its equivalent **present value** by the appropriate **discount factor**, which is sensitive to the **interest rate**.

The exposition of the multi-period household budget constraint makes clear that changes in economic variables such as real wages, asset prices, and interest rates have complex effects on consumption. These are broken down into **income effects, substitution effects and intertemporal substitution effects.** Finally, these effects can be aggregated across individuals to produce **aggregates** of consumption and investment.

Chapter Outline:

I. Introduction: Consumption and Saving

II. Consumption in a 2 Period Model.
- A. Present Value and Discount Factors
- B. Income effects
- C. Intertemporal Substitution Effects
- D. Combined Effects

III. Consumption Over Many Years

A. The Multiyear Budget Constraint
B. Temporary and Permanent Income
i. the propensity to consume

IV. Consumption, Saving, and Investment in Equilibrium
A. Aggregate Household Budget Constraint

V. Summary

Teaching Tips:

1. Provide numerical examples early and often until students gain confidence using these budget constraints. Students will more easily relate to the two period model, so this should be used extensively before moving on the the multi-period constraint described later in the chapter.

2. Milt Marquis of The Federal Reserve Bank of San Francisco has issued a brief analysis of the declining U.S. savings rate that can help students understand the the relationship of saving rates and changes in wealth. Although stocks and residential housing are not included in the simplified model, they play a significant role in U.S. wealth accumulation. The graph below should provoke interesting discussion. The entire article can be found at http://www.frbsf.org/publications/economics/letter/2002/el2002-09.html.

Figure 1: NIPA Personal Saving Rate and Household Financial Wealth / DPI

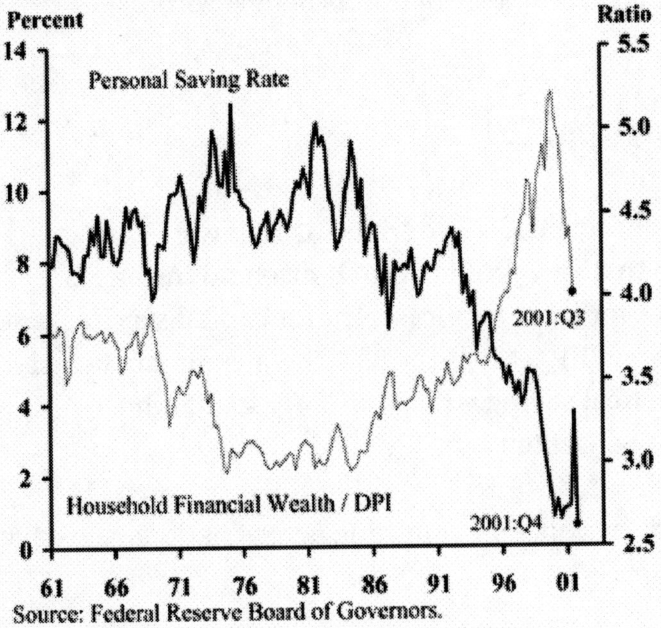

Source: Federal Reserve Board of Governors.

3. It is important for students to understand how savings is related to real asset accumulation over time. A fair amount of time should be spent discussing the figure 7.2 (again using numerical examples). The way in which wealth is presented here is highly simplified. Be sure students understand that the variables i, R, and K are symbolic of a much more complex reality. For example, although there is no explicit modeling of capital gains in this model, those gains are implicit in the rate of return on capital ownership, R/P. The case of residential housing is particularly interesting, since the rate of return is in the *implicit* value of rental services supplied.

4. One way for students to keep track of the differences between income and substitution effects is to note that substitution effects always involve the reduction of one activity at the expense of another, intertemporal substitution effects always involve the increase of one variable at the expense of another in a different time period, and income effects will produce increases in all variables or decreases in all variables.

5. The assumption that the substitution effect dominates is problematic for an open economy of net savers. Discuss how a change in the interest rate might affect the consumption decisions of a retired couple living off of their assets. Now extend that analysis to discuss what the aggregate effects of changing interest rates in a country with a high national savings rate, like Japan. Contrast that with the predicted behavior of a net borrower nation, like the U.S. At the end of the discussion emphasize that in a closed economy, a nation can not be a net borrower or a net saver, so that the balance of bonds held is zero.

Answers to review questions, pg. 169

1. The two year household budget constraint is derived as follows:
Assuming that markets clear(so that real profit =zero) household income is generated in our model by wages for labor services, rent for capital services, and interest on bonds. Real income = (w/P)*L + i*(B/P + K). The income can be used for consumption or real saving. Real saving = (1/P)*◎B + ◎K so that the household budget constraint can be written:

C+(1/P)*◎B + ◎K= +(w/P)*L + i*(B/P + K) (eq. 7.1)

Adding subscripts to denote each period, and summing across periods, we have:

$$C_1 + (B_1/P + K_1) - (B_0/P + K_0) = +(w/P)_1{*}L + i_0{*}(B_0/P + K_0) \quad \text{(eq. 7.2)}$$

Subtracting consumption and initial assets from both sides yields:

$$(B_1/P + K_1) = +(w/P)_1{*}L + i_0{*}(B_0/P + K_0) + (B_0/P + K_0) - C_1 \quad \text{(eq. 7.4)}$$

Or simply

$$(B_1/P + K_1) = +(w/P)_1{*}L + (1+i_0){*}(B_0/P + K_0) - C_1 \quad \text{(7.4a)}$$

By a similar procedure, we can rewrite the the budget constraint in period 2 as:

$$(B_2/P + K_2) = +(w/P)_2{*}L + (1+i_1){*}(B_1/P + K_1) - C_2 \quad \text{(7.5a)}$$

Substituting 7.4a into 7.5a yields:

$$(B_2/P + K_2) = (w/P)_2{*}L + (1+i_1){*}[(w/P)_1{*}L + (1+i_0){*}(B_0/P + K_0) - C_1] - C_2$$

Dividing both sides by $(1+i_i)$ rearranging terms to group consumption on the left hand side yields:

$$C_1 + C_2/(1+i_1) = (w/P)_1{*}L + (w/P)_2{*}L/(1+i_1) + (1+i_0){*}(B_0/P + K_0) - (B_2/P + K_2)/(1+i_1)$$

Which is equation (7.9), the two period budget constraint.

2. When we use the present value, we multiply the number by a discount factor $(1/(/(1+i_i))$ which is less than 1 for any positive rate of interest. A positive rate of interest is due to several factors, including the fact that consumers are generally impatient, (in economics jargon, they have a positive rate of time preference), there are opportunity costs associated with waiting(namely, interest income foregone) and is waiting is associated with increased risk.

3. Propensity to consume is determined in our model by a rational choice, by which we mean that consumers seek to maximize their utility across periods. Assuming that *consumption smoothing* over time yields higher total utility, the consumer will tend to spread the benefits of a temporary increase over time. Therefore, the propensity to consume out of temporary increases in income is much less than 1. The propensity to consume out of permanent increases in income is approximately 1. A propensity to consume out of additional income greater than one is unlikely, given the consumption smoothing assumption.

4. Effect on this year's consumption:

a. an increase in the interest rate has an ambiguous impact on current consumption of a household; by the *substitution effect,* it would reduce it. But if our consumer is a net saver, it may increase it by the *income effect*. If the consumer is a net borrower, then both effects would lead to a reduction in current consumption. (For the aggregate level of consumption, the income effect would be zero, since net saving in a closed economy must be zero).

b. Consumption would increase by approximately ◎(w/P)L.

c. Consumption would increase, but only by a fraction of ◎ (w/P)L.

d. Consumption would increase, but only by a fraction of ◎ $(w/P)L$.
e. Consumption would increase, but only by a fraction of the ◎ $(B_0/P + K_0)$.

Answers to Problems for discussion, pg. 169

5. a)In order to keep the notation somewhat manageable, we will make the simplifying assumption that interest rates are constant.
Then permanent income = $(1+i)((B_0/P + K_0) + L^*$ ◎◎$_{t=1}(w/P)_t/(1+i)^t$
Where T represents the number of periods of earned income. Permanent income in this case, consists in the value of assets in period one plus the sum of the discounted real wages earned.
b) The permanent household budget constraint is given by:

◎◎$_{t=1}C_t/(1+i)^t = (1+i)((B_0/P + K_0) + L^*$ ◎◎$_{t=1}(w/P)_t/(1+i)^t$, which implies a propensity to consume =1. (permanent consumption=permanent income)

c) Permanent income in that case is given by C◎◎$_{t=1}1/(1+i)^t$, where C is the amount consumed in each period. (If the time horizon is very long, this number converges to C/i.) For example, if consumption is 10,000 per month and the interest rate is 1% per month, then permanent income over a period of 50 years (600 months) is approximately 10,000/.01 or $1,000,000.

6.a) If the household has a positive balance of bonds, it is a net saver to begin with. The real value of the asset is B_0/P, so the higher price level P reduces the real value of the asset. If there is no offsetting increase in w, (the nominal wage) then permanent labor income will also be reduced. Both of these changes result in lower permanent income and a lower rate of consumption in each period. If the nominal balance is zero, the income effect will still be negative. However, if the balance is negative, the consumer is a net borrower, and the increase in the price level reduces the real value of their debt, which results in a higher permanent income and consumption rate.

b) The assumption that $B_0=0$ means that the only impact is on the stream of labor income. A higher interest rate reduces the present value of the income stream and reduces permanent income, which should reduce the rate of consumption.

Chapter 8: An Equilibrium Business Cycle Model

Chapter Summary:

This chapter provides a "real" business cycle model that will serve as the basis for constructing each of the alternative theories described in subsequent chapters. The key assumption here is one of flexible prices so that all markets clear. Fluctuations in GDP and employment are caused by temporary technological shocks which change the marginal product of resources. This sets in motion a series of adjustments which matches closely the real world data on business cycles. A temporary technological improvement leads to increased marginal productivity of resources, and cause the demand for labor and capital services to increase. This produces procyclical variations in real wages, interest rates, and output. The temporary nature of the shock generates relatively mild procyclical movements in consumption, but relatively large procyclical changes in investment. At the end of the chapter, the assumption of fixed labor supply is dropped in favor of a more rational labor supply function which depends on real wages and interest rates. The income effects and intertemporal substitution effects of changes in the interest rate and real wages produce procyclical variations in employment.

Chapter Outline:

I. Cyclical Behavior of Real GDP-Recessions and Booms
   A. Conceptual Issues
   B. The Model
      i. The marginal product of labor and the real wage rate
      ii. Marginal product of capital, real rental price and the interest rate
      iii. Consumption and Investment
   A. The Real Wage Rate
   B. The Real Rental Price
   C. The Interest Rate

II. Temporary Changes in the Technology Level

III. Variation in Labor Input
   A. Labor Supply
      i. The Substitution effect for leisure and consumption
      ii. Income effects on labor supply
      iii. Intertemporal-substitution effects on labor supply
   A. Fluctuations in Labor Input
      a. The cyclical behavior of labor input: empirical
      b. The cyclical behavior of labor input: theory
      c. The cyclical behavior of labor productivity

Teaching Tips:

1. Review the patterns reviewed by business cycle data with students. Make them aware that the efforts of economists to develop a model capable of explaining and predicting these movements have not yet formed a consensus. But a consensus emerged regarding the importance of basing the theory on sound microeconomic foundations. This model is one of the first to fully incorporate the insights of microeconomic theory to explain movement in macroeconomic aggregates.

2. One of the interesting aspects of this model is the ability to generate a business cycle which is completely independent of monetary influences. As we will see in later chapters, variations in the nominal money supply or demand have no real effects in this model.

3. A historical perspective would be helpful to students see the logic of the equilibrium business cycle theory. A discussion of figure 8.4 is useful, but some context for students unfamiliar with U.S. economic history might help. This article by Wall Street Journal reporter Bob Davis can provide students with that context: "History Lessons: Past Crises Offer Hope for Economy" (WSJ, page A1, September 26, 2002.)

4. Students understand positive technological shocks, but find negative shocks difficult to envision. Emphasize that these "shocks" could have other sources beyond technological change. The recent example of Hurricane Katrina and its impact on the capital stock of the Gulf Coast region provides a recent example. In cases like this, the productivity shock comes from damage to the capital stock. On the other hand, regulatory policies and trade policies can have similar impact on productivity. Consider France's move to the 35 hour work week, the Family Leave Act, or even a Tariff increase that might reduce trade and the gains from comparative advantage that accompany it. If we think about the parameter "A" as "total factor productivity", we can imagine a much broader range of productivity shocks.

5. Real business cycle theory is dynamic- the modeling techniques used are somewhat beyond the range of students enrolled in the course. But instructors should note that it may be useful to think of "a decrease in GDP" as a "decrease in the *growth rate* of GDP." Figures 8.3 and 8.4 which show deviations from trend growth rates can be used to make this point.

Answers to review questions, pg. 199

1. This year's labor supplied depends on the leisure consumed. We would expect that market events would have at least one of 3 potential effects: income effects, substitution effects, or intertemporal substitution effects.

a. Higher interest rates primarily cause an intertemporal substitution effect: the opportunity cost of current leisure becomes is higher, so current leisure should fall and current labor supply should increase.

b. A permanent increase in the real wage rate will have both an income and substitution effect. On the one hand, people can afford more leisure (income effect) which would reduce the current labor supply. On the other hand, the opportunity cost of current leisure has risen (substitution effect) which would tend to reduce current labor supplied. The net effect is ambiguous.

c. A temporary increase in the real wage rate is similar to part b above. However, in this case, since the higher wages will not persist, the income effect will not be as large, and we would expect the substitution effect to dominate. We would also observe an intertemporal substitution effect, since the current wage is higher relative to future wages. This would cause an increase in current labor supplied.

d. A one time windfall produces an income effect only. Leisure will increase and labor supply will decrease, both in the current and subsequent periods.

B. Problems for discussion, pg. 199-200

2. a. Labor force participation rates should respond to changes in the real wage rate just as the quantity of labor supplied does. In this case, the real wage was increasing throughout the period, so we should see an increase in labor supply due to the substitution effect. However, the income effect would depress labor participation rates. (Income effects would not influence the decision of a single person not currently in the labor force, since their current income from wages is zero, but it could affect the working spouse of a married person. It also could allow someone to delay entry or retire at an earlier age.) The data suggests that the income effect dominates the substitution effect over this period.

b. The fact that the average work week did not change implies that the labor supply of working individuals is inelastic with respect to the real wage. This hard to reconcile with the data on labor force participation, which indicates a strong substitution effect. However, if we consider labor supplied by households rather than individuals, the results are more consistent. In this case, the average two-earner household is supplying more labor in response to the higher real wage rate.

c. We see that when we consider the labor supply decision of households, rather than individuals, that we can reconcile the data found in parts a and b. However, this does not work when dealing with the labor supply decisions of single people. We would expect both the average work hours and the labor force participation rates to increase if the changes are caused by the substitution effect. However, other factors, such as changing cultural norms about the role of women in society, would have a potentially strong impact, which could result in higher participation rates while leaving the average work week unchanged.

3. A reduction in the labor force:

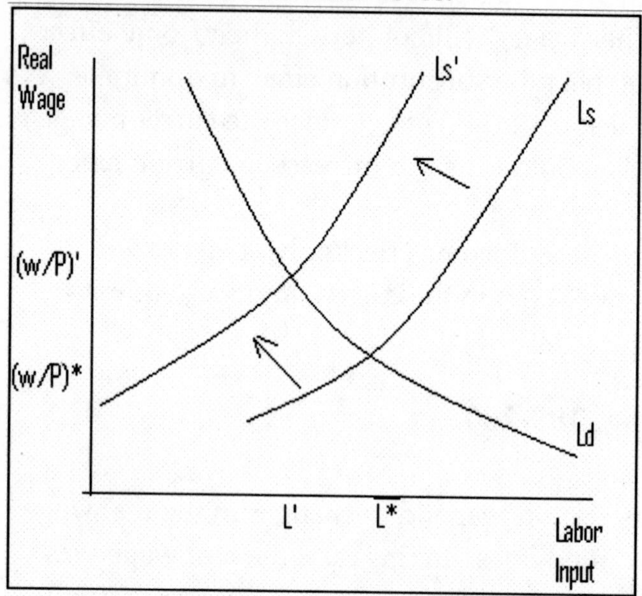

A decrease in population shifts the labor supply curve to the left. This causes an increase in equilibrium real wages and a decrease in equilibrium real output. (These effects on the wage may be offset somewhat by other factors. First, the higher real wage may result in more hours of labor provided by each worker due to the substitution effect. we could also see effects on the labor supply curve due to possible reductions in interest rates, as in part b below).

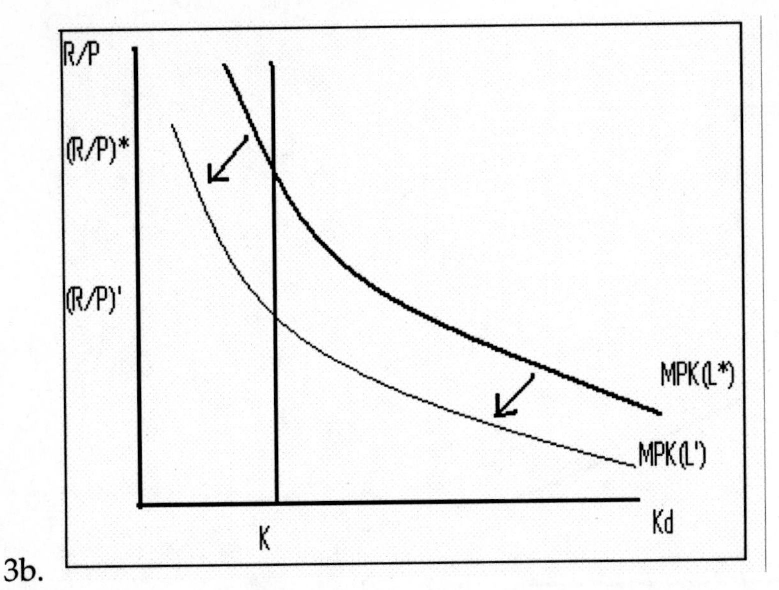

3b.

A reduction in labor per unit of capital reduces the marginal product of capital and causes the MPK curve to shift left from MPK(L) to MPK(L').*
The real rental rate of capital falls from (R/P) to (R/P)'.*

3c. If we continue to assume constant returns to scale in the production function, then it can be shown that output per worker (y) increases as the capital per worker (k) increases. Since the population reduction is permanent, both current and future incomes are affected, so that the marginal propensity to consume out of current income will be approximately 1. On the other hand, we also have an intertemporal substitution due to the relative reduction in the real rental rate of capital. The effect will be to reduce interest rates, which should reduce increase current consumption further. The combined effects indicate that consumption per worker will increase by more than the change in income per worker. In the aggregate, consumption my decrease because there are fewer consumers, but the aggregate change in consumption is less than the aggregate change in income. For the impact on aggregate investment, refer to Equation 7.13 : ◎K =Y-C-+◎K. The preceding analysis implies that the right hand side of this equation will be negative, and the capital stock will decline over time.

4. A reduction in the capital stock:

4a.

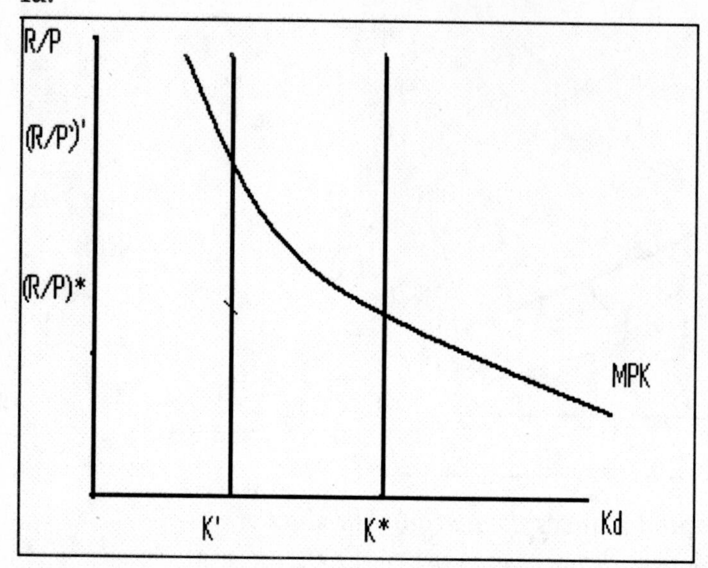

The capital stock declines from K to K'; the MPK increases from MPK* to MPK', and the interest rate should increase in response to higher marginal return on capital investment.*

4b.

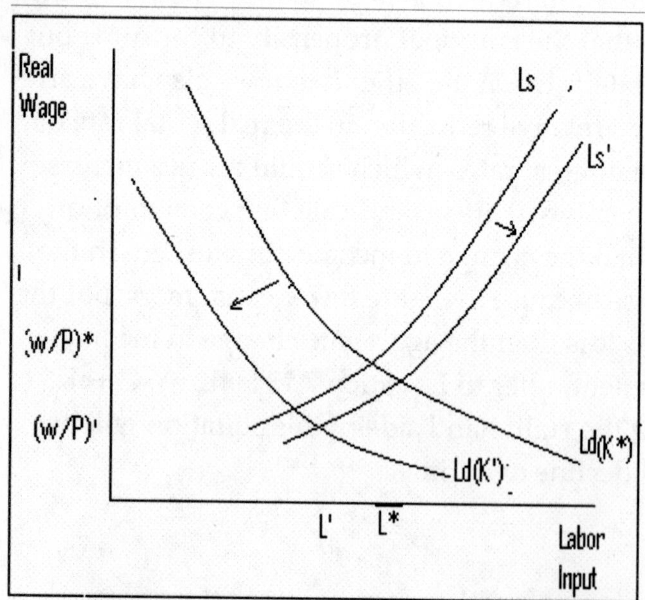

The capital per worker decreases, reducing the marginal product of labor and shifting the labor demand curve to the left. The higher interest rates cause the current labor supply to shift the the right.

The real wage falls from (w/P) to (w/P)' and labor input falls from L* to L'.*

4c. In this case, we have the opposite effects found in part 3c; income per worker falls, and consumption per worker will fall for two reasons: the decrease in income as well as the intertemporal substitution effect. The net effect is a decrease in aggregate consumption which is greater than the decrease in current income: the capital stock will increase over time.

5. A Reduction in Desired Saving

5a. Since the reduction in the desired savings rate has no effect on labor productivity, the demand for labor will not change. There will be no *direct* effects on labor supply. However, since the reduced savings rate will have the effect of increasing interest rates (see part 5b), the opportunity cost of current leisure will increase, and the labor supply curve will shift to the right (intertemporal substitution effect). This chain of events would cause real wages to fall and labor input to rise.

5b. A decrease in savings rates would cause an excess supply of bonds in the market, which would raise interest rates. In the graph for capital services, In we will assume that the supply of capital is fixed in the current period. Later, in chapter 9, we will relax this assumption somewhat to allow for different capital utilization rates. The marginal product of capital is determined by the level of technology and the labor force. As we saw in part 5a, there might be a slight increase in labor input which would cause the MPK curve to shift to the right. This would result in higher real rental rates on capital services. This is consistent with the notion that in equilibrium, both interest rates and the real rental rate on capital must be equal.

5c. Aggregate consumption increases, investment falls. The lower rate of investment will cause the capital stock to grow more slowly or even decrease over time. This is especially true if the intertemporal substitution effect described in 5a and 5b is too small to restore equilibrium in the asset markets. In that case, the additional labor does not increase MPK enough, and the only alternative is for the supply of capital to fall. This would require negative net investment.

6. A willingness to work more.

6a. The direct effect of this change would be to shift the supply curve of labor to the right; real wages fall and labor input increases.

6b. The increase in labor seen in part 6a would cause the MPK curve to shift to the right, resulting in higher real rental rates for capital. In response, interest rates would rise to maintain the equality in the real rates of return to bonds and capital. This rise in the interest rate would have the indirect effect of increasing current labor supply even further, because it raises the opportunity cost of current leisure.

6c. The level of consumption will rise due to the increase in permanent income, but the substitution effect of higher interest rates will ensure that some of the additional income will be devoted to increasing investment. The capital stock will increase.

Chapter 9: Capital Utilization and Unemployment

Chapter Summary:

This chapter provides a more realistic treatment of resource markets in relation to the business cycle. The procyclical pattern of **capacity utilization** is explained in terms of a depreciation function, where higher rates of capacity utilization are associated with higher rates of depreciation. Higher rental rates for capital services generate higher rates of capacity utilization. Attention then turns to the labor market, where the **natural rate of unemployment** is explained as equilibrium between job finding and job search rates. Changes in the real wage generate increase rates of job finding, and helps to explain the highly cyclical nature of employment.

Chapter Outline:

I. Capital Input
   - A. The Demand for Capital Services
   - B. The Supply of Capital Services
   - C. Marketing Clearing and Capital Utilization
   - D. The Cyclical of Capacity Utilization

II. The Labor Force, Employment, and Unemployment
   - A. Basic Concepts and Empirical Patterns
   - B. A Model of Job Finding
   - C. Search by Firms
   - D. Job Separation
   - E. Job Separations, Jon Finding and the Natural Unemployment Rate
   - F. Economic Fluctuation, Employment, and Unemployment
   - G. Vacancies

Teaching Tips:

1. The famous scene in "Gone with the Wind" in which Scarlett O'Hara whips her horse to death in her rush to get back to her family home in Tara provides a vivid illustration of why businesses may not want to utilize 100% of their resource capacity.

2. The "Back to Reality" feature on page 206 which provides many concrete examples of how costs rise as capacity utilization approaches 100%. Instructors

can generate a lively discussion by encouraging students to come up with other examples based on their own work experience.

3. A discussion of the search theory of labor markets can be energized by asking for a show of hands of students who would like to be married. Then ask those whose hands are up to keep them up if they currently are married. There will be a dramatic difference. Ask them if they believe this discrepancy is the result of "involuntary" or "involuntary" decisions. This can lead into all kinds of discussions about the nature of unemployment (is there such a thing as "involuntary unemployment"?), imperfect information, the role of technology in reducing search costs, etc.

4. A discussion of international differences in the natural rates of unemployment is a useful way to help students distinguish between natural and cyclical unemployment. Explain why a "hire and fire" society like the U.S. might have a lower natural rate of unemployment than many Western European countries that have a higher degree of job security due to unionization and labor laws which reduce job separation. The only explanation lies in the "job finding" rate: legal restrictions on wages, collective bargaining, and generous unemployment benefits and social insurance programs all point toward a smaller job finding rate.

5. The bathtub provides a suitable illustration for employment as a function of job finding (the faucet) and job separation (the drain) leading to variations in employment (the water level).

6. The "jobless recovery" is a term used to describe a period of expansion when unemployment rates remain stubbornly high. The persistence of high unemployment rates should be explained using the hypothetical example in table 9.2 on page 225.

Answers to review questions, pg. 229

1. Machines are determined by the capital stock available during the period, and may be considered a "fixed" input; but the number of hours used is a "variable" input and can be adjusted according to current conditions. Thus, the actual capital input is the number of machines multiplied by the number of hours each is used. Equation 9.4 shows that the rate of return on capital ownership is not just a function of machines owned, but of the number of machine hours supplied.

Since the rate of depreciation increases with the intensity of use, the rate of return to capital ownership can be reduced by using it too intensely.

2. a. An increase in R/P increases the value of each hour of capital supplied.
   b. If the effects of capacity utilization rates on depreciation were to increase, then the net rate of return would be reduced for all values of ⊚.

3. The unemployment rate is the number of unemployed/labor force. Since the labor force is weakly pro-cyclical, the numbers will underestimate the true unemployment rate as the economy approaches a trough of a recession (when labor force is smaller) and overestimate it during the initial stages of recovery. (See discussion of # 9 below.)

4. The major reason a worker may reject an offer of employment which is greater than their current income is that the offer is in the lower end of the distribution of expected offers. If they refuse, they must suffer the opportunity costs associated with the foregone wages, but in return, they might end up find a better offer that more than makes up for it. It is the tradeoff between these two opportunities that determines the reservation wage: the lowest acceptable offer.

5. Job separations may have a variety of causes including:
   - imperfect information: either the job or the employee mail fail to live up to the expectations based on the original evaluation.
   - circumstances of the job may change: technology or market demands may change in a way that reduces the value of the worker to the firm.
   - circumstances of the worker may change: the worker may have a child or family member needing care, they may develop different preferences regarding location or working conditions, etc.
   - Some jobs are temporary by design, including seasonal work.

6. The natural rate of unemployment is the rate associated with a balanced flows of job finding and job separations. The actual rate of unemployment will vary from the natural rate when temporary "shocks" occur that temporarily change the rate of job finding, job separation, or both. The natural rate will be affected by institutional changes that change the job search. For example, the use of the internet allows information to flow more rapidly between firms and workers, resulting in lower search times. A reduction in unemployment benefits could also motivate workers to reduce search times; tenure laws could reduce the rate of job separation, etc.

Answers to problems for discussion, pg. 230

7:

event:	effect on job-finding rate:	effect on duration of unemployment:
increase in unemployment insurance benefits	reduce	increase
increase in unemployment insurance duration	reduce	increase
technological change that improves matching	increase	reduce

8. The natural rate of unemployment seems to be 4.76%, as seen in the following table:

time	employment	unemployment	separation	finding	u. rate:
0	92	8	1.84	3.2	0.08
1	93.36	6.64	1.8672	2.656	0.0664
2	94.1488	5.8512	1.882976	2.34048	0.058512
3	94.606304	5.393696	1.8921261	2.1574784	0.053937
4	94.871656	5.12834368	1.8974331	2.0513375	0.051283
5	95.025561	4.974439334	1.9005112	1.9897757	0.049744
6	95.114825	4.885174814	1.9022965	1.9540699	0.048852
7	95.166599	4.833401392	1.903332	1.9333606	0.048334
8	95.196627	4.803372807	1.9039325	1.9213491	0.048034
9	95.214044	4.785956228	1.9042809	1.9143825	0.04786
10	95.224145	4.775854612	1.9044829	1.9103418	0.047759
11	95.230004	4.769995675	1.9046001	1.9079983	0.0477
12	95.233403	4.766597492	1.9046681	1.906639	0.047666
13	95.235373	4.764626545	1.9047075	1.9058506	0.047646
14	95.236517	4.763483396	1.9047303	1.9053934	0.047635
15	95.23718	4.76282037	1.9047436	1.9051281	0.047628

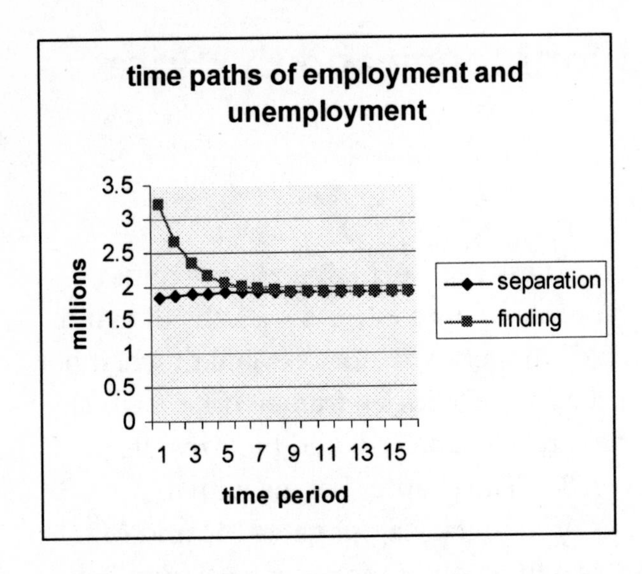

9. Unemployed persons not "actively seeking work" are not counted in the labor force. It may be that some of them are not seeking work until business conditions improve, that is, until the expected probability (and therefore, the net benefits) of the job search increase. In this case, the labor force would be pro-cyclical, and the unemployment rates would decrease during a recession not because people are finding jobs, but because they have stopped looking for them. These people are officially designated as "discouraged workers". When business conditions pick up and these "discouraged workers" begin actively looking for work again, their presence in the labor force would tend to push unemployment rates up again. On the other hand, if one person in a household loses a job or suffers a loss of income, another member of the household not currently in the labor force may decide to enter in an effort to maintain household income.

10. New technology should increase the marginal product of labor, creating new job offers. Job offers would be pro-cyclical in this case. When there are more vacancies, the job search will likely be shorter and the unemployment rates lower. Therefore, the unemployment rate would be countercyclical and the graph of vacancies vs. unemployment rates will show an inverse relationship, as in figure 9.12.

Chapter 10: The Demand for Money and the Price Level

Chapter Summary:

In the equilibrium theory of the business cycle explained in previous chapters, money has played an important role. This contrasts with the demand side theories of the business cycle in which monetary factors explain much, if not all of the variability in real GDP. This chapter provides a framework by which alternative theories of the business cycle can be examined, and their results compared to the equilibrium model of ch.8. The chapter begins with a description of money and the definitions of **monetary aggregates M1 and M2.** **Demand for money** based is described as a function of the price level, nominal interest rates and real GDP,Y. Money demand is directly related to the price level and real GDP and inversely related to interest rates, which represent an opportunity cost of holding money. The **money supply** is assumed to be determined as a matter of policy by the central bank. It is the equilibrium between money supply and demand that generates the price level in the economy. Shocks can originate on the supply side or the demand side, but they have no effect on any "real" variables, only the price level – this demonstrates the **neutrality of money** in the equilibrium business cycle model. A discussion of monetary policy follows, and it is shown that **price level targeting** generates a theory of **endogenous money** supply. The difficulty of accommodating the money supply to achieve this target in a world of cyclical and seasonal variations in money demand is discussed.

Chapter Outline:

I. Concepts of Money

II. The Demand for Money
   - A. The Interest Rate and the Demand for Money
   - B. The Price Level and the Demand for Money
   - C. Real GDP and the Demand for Money
   - D. Other Influences on the Demand for Money
   - E. The Money-Demand Function
   - F. Empirical on the Demand for Money

III. Determination of the Price Level

A. The Nominal Quantity of Money Supplied Equals the Nominal Quantity Demanded
B. A change in the Nominal Quantity of Money
C. The Neutrality of Money
D. The Cyclical Behavior of the Price Level
E. Price-Level Targeting and Endogenous Money
    i. Trend growth of money
    ii. Cyclical behavior of money
    iii. Seasonal variations in money

Teaching Tips:

1. An interesting development in the evolution of money is the use of currencies in the virtual reality worlds created by internet gaming. In this case, virtual money is being used to buy virtual goods. The fact that this virtual currency is now trading for real currency provides an example of how technological change is making it difficult for monetary authorities to keep up with the markets. You may want your students to read the following article on the subject: "QQ: China's New Coin of the Realm? Officials Try To Crack Down As Fake Online Currency Is Traded for Real Money" Wall Street Journal, Mar. 30, 2007 pg. B1.

2. The shape of the money demand curve in figure 10.1 is unlike any other demand curve the student has studied: it slopes upward! Make sure students interpret it correctly. It may also be helpful as an exercise to have them diagram the same market using 1/P on the vertical axis. Help them to interpret this reciprocal as the "price of money".

3. Asking students to articulate their own reasons for holding currency can be a productive way to help them relate to the theory of money demand. A quick survey of the class will reveal that most of them have a debit card. Has the debit card increased or reduced the average balance of currency in their wallet? Ask them to explain this result in terms of transaction costs.

4. Early in their lives my grandparents (and many others, I suspect) used an "envelope" budgeting system. They literally put cash from their paychecks into an envelopes marked "food", "rent", "entertainment" and so on. When they spent less on food than they had budgeted, they put the remainder in an envelope marked "savings". Ask students to explain why this particular money

management strategy made sense for the time, and invite them to speculate how money management strategies of the future may differ from our own.

Answers to review questions, pg. 254

1. If you keep your wealth in a portfolio of assets, the major transaction costs will be in the transfer of wealth from one account to another. The costs of making this transfer include travel time and expense, waiting in line, payment of relevant fees charged by the institution. This has become much more convenient as technology has evolved. The telephone, fax machine, atm machine, and the internet have brought these costs down dramatically in the last few decades.

2. a. An increase in the nominal interest rate raises the opportunity cost of holding money; demand will decrease.
   b. An increase in real transactions costs makes it more difficult to convert wealth into purchasing power, demand for money as a means of exchange will increase.
   c. An increase in real GDP caused by increased per-capita income will increase the demand for money.
   d. An increase in real GDP caused by population growth will increase the demand for money.
   e. An increase in the price level will increase the demand for money.

3. a. A one time doubling will reduce the real wage only if nominal wages are constant. If nominal wages also double, then the real wage will not change.
   b. As in part 3a, an increase in the nominal wage will only help the worker if prices do not increase as well.
   c. Money neutrality holds if nominal values change in proportion, so that real values are unaffected. Obviously if both nominal wages and prices double, then the real labor employed, real output, and real labor income will not change.

4. The quantity theory of money cannot be supported by theoretical arguments alone. The theory suggests that changes in money demand can affect the price level even when the nominal money stock is fixed. The quantity theory then becomes an argument that the demand for money is relatively stable over the long run. This assumption would have to be tested by examining the behavior of money demand over the long run. (Ironically, the behavior of money demand did appear to change during the 1980's just as many central banks had begun targeting the nominal money supply as a policy instrument.)

5. A favorable productivity shock increases the demand for labor resulting in a higher level of employment and output. A higher level of output generates an increase in money demand, which would cause the price level to drop as in the diagram. The monetary authorities could counter with an increase in the money supply to maintain the current price level at its target level, P* as in the diagram below:

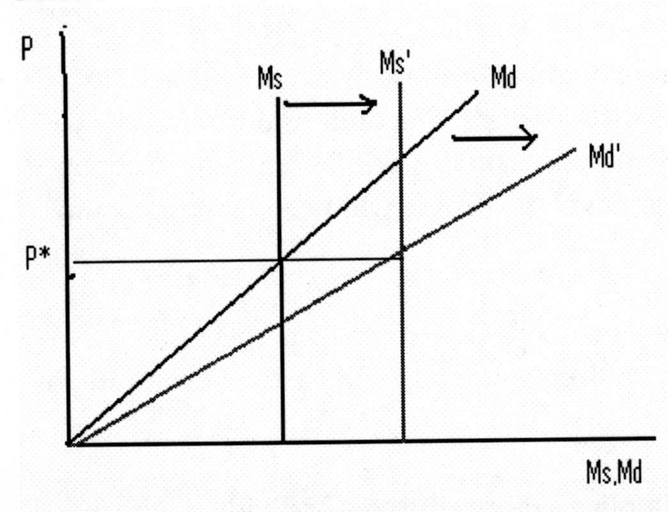

6. Increases in money supply tend to raise prices, while increases in the demand for money have the opposite effect. If both supply and demand for money were increasing, the results for P would be ambiguous, depending on the relative changes in the demand and the supply. If they are changing in proportion, then there will be no the price level. In any case, the change in price will only affect nominal GDP; leaving real GDP unchanged.

7. "Endogenous money" implies that changes in the demand for money will cause predictable changes in the supply of money. In that case, the supply of money is determined by factors within the model. If the monetary authorities choose to respond to changes in the money demand with similar changes in the supply of money, then factors which lead to increased demand for money will also lead to increased supply of money. For example, if real GDP, Y were to increase, then the demand for money would increase. Money supply would also increase. There would be a positive correlation between money supply and real GDP, but the change in money supply would be an effect, not the cause of increase in GDP.

Answers to problems for discussion, pg. 255-257

8. The answers to of these questions are true.

a. True. One reason is that more production in an agricultural society is for home use, not to be sold on the market. The division of labor and structure of production is not as complex, resulting in fewer transactions for a given level of production. Fewer transactions means less demand for money.

b. True. Liquidity provides more options for those attempting to escape persecution which is more likely in dictatorships. The underground economy is likely to be larger. It is more likely that the economy will be a planned economy, in which case shortages are likely to develop. People will need money "just in case" goods become available.

c. True. If the elderly are more dependent on income from their assets, which are "liquidated" during their retirement. They will have a higher ratio of monetary transactions to income.

d. True. Higher literacy rate implies a more educated individual who is likely to keep more wealth in interest bearing assets because they know how to manage them.

9. See graph:

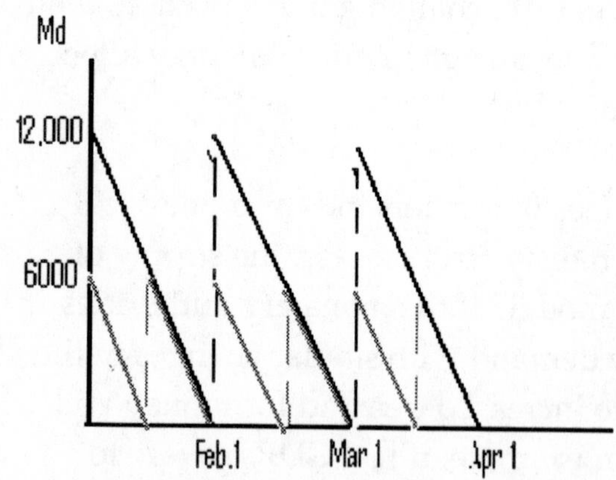

a. The large triangles show that the cash balance is 12,000 at the first of each month and gradually falls to zero by the end of the month. (The graph shows the first three months). Average money balance is 6000, which corresponds to the quantity of money demanded in our model.

b. See the smaller triangles in the graph. Average money holdings fall to $3000.

c. The higher level of consumption would result in an average monthly balance of $12,000. In this case, the opportunity cost of interest foregone has increased, but transactions costs have not. Therefore, a more active money management strategy is called for (due to economies of scale).

10. One way to approach these problems is to refer to an equation for velocity such as this: V=Y/L, where Y is real GDP and L is real money demand.

a. Higher values for i reduce real money demand; V increases.

b. An increase in Y leads to an increase in V.

c. Similar to (b); there will be an increase in V. The change in V in this case might be slightly less due to economies of scale in money management. In other words, people in part b would have larger real money balances. Economies of scale would reduce the transactions cost of shifting between money and other assets, and therefore the overall demand for money might be lower in part (b), which implies V would be slightly higher.

d. Since P does not change the demand for real money balances, there should be no change in velocity. (However, inflation would have an effect on money demand and velocity because it would reduce L).

e. Nominal GDP measures current income in dollars, but the desired volume of transactions depends on wealth as well as income.

f. As an economy develops, financial institutions become more sophisticated and convenient, portfolio management becomes more important and related transactions costs fall. All of this has the effect of reducing the real demand for money; Y and L increase over time, but L will grow more slowly; V increases.

11. a. 24 payments imply $2500 per payment. Assuming a constant rate of purchasing this implies an average money balance of approximately $1250.

b. 12 payments imply $5000 per payment, average balance =$2500.

c. There is an inverse relationship between the two; less frequent payments result in higher money demand.

d. An interest bearing savings account is not "money" in our classification; therefore it would reduce the demand for money.

12. a. Your assumptions about the timing of the shopping trip will affect your answer; if you shop on the first day of the month and once every seven or eight days following, your average balance will be approximately $1900. Comparing this to part (b) of question 11 shows that the average money balance has fallen. This is because a large chunk of money is spent immediately on its receipt.

b. The money balance would fall further (to $1250) because an even larger share of money is spent prior to the actual consumption of goods.

c. The fewer trips, the smaller the money demand. In an extreme case, someone could do all their shopping on the day of their pay check, which would imply a zero average balance for the month.

d. Less frequent trips; implies smaller money demand.

13. a. It may be treated as an increase in real income, just as if prices had fallen.

b. The income effect is positive on both consumption and leisure.

c. The effects would be similar.

14. a. The price level should fall to 1/10 of its current level. The interest rate will not change.

b. There is no change in any real variable.

c. Yes, only the price level has changed in response to the currency reform. (One could argue that there are "menu costs" associated with these price changes that would reduce real GDP, but these are likely to be relatively insignificant.)

15. a. There is a direct relationship between denomination and P.

b. The demand for "big ticket items" like jewelry and cars may increase. These purchases will be easier to transact in large denomination bills.

c. No obvious relationship.

d. Higher denominations may be desired for large cash transactions, such as you might expect in the underground economy. It is easier to fit $20,000 in a briefcase using $100 bills rather than singles. (Not to mention quicker to count!)

e. Foreigners would not likely use U.S. currency for routine transactions. It would be more likely to be treated as an asset, in which case large denominations are more convenient.

It is difficult to understand why the denominations did not grow more rapidly prior to 1970, since most of the items lean in that direction. Perhaps it was the inflation and the rapid expansion of the drug trade in the 1970's and beyond that led the increase. In many countries, the holding of U.S. currency was not permitted until recently.

Chapter 11: Inflation, Money Growth, and Interest Rates

Chapter Summary:

The chapter attempts to explain the relationship between inflation, money growth and interest rates using the tools of equilibrium business cycle theory and the theory of money supply and demand developed in previous chapters. It begins by examining the international data on inflation rates and establishes the link between nominal monetary growth and inflation rates. Then the chapter describes the impact of inflation on interest rates. There are two distinctions which are important for understanding this particular section: actual versus expected interest rates, and real versus nominal interest rates. It is shown that intertemporal substitution effects depend on the expected real interest rate, something that cannot be directly observed. 3 different approaches to measuring expected values for inflation and interest rates are described, including the use of inflation indexed bonds.

In the previous chapter, changes in the amount of money had no effects on real variables- the analysis in this chapter demonstrates that changes in the growth rates of money also have no real effects.

The difference between the growth rate of the money supply and money demand determines the rate of inflation. Changes in the growth rate of money are shown to cause rapid changes in the price level; the mere anticipation of the change can cause the price level to "jump". The section shows how this "jump" is related to the theory of money demand.

The last section discusses how growth in the money supply can generate changes in the real revenue of government, unless money demand falls drastically as a consequence. An extensive discussion of the issue using the German hyperinflation is discussed in the "by the numbers" example on page 285.

Chapter Outline:

I. Cross Country Data on Inflation and Money Growth

II. Inflation and Interest Rates

A. Actual and Expected Inflation

B. Real and Nominal Interest Rates

C. The Real Interest Rate and Intertemporal Substitution

D. Actual and Expected Real Interest Rates
   i. Measuring expected inflation
   ii. U.S expected inflation and inflation and interest since WW II
   iii. Indexed bonds, real interest rates, and expected inflation rates

III. Inflation in the Equilibrium Business-Cycle Model
   A. Intertemporal-Substitution Effects
   B. Bonds and Capital
   C. Interest Rates and the Demands for Money
   D. Inflation and the Real Economy
   E. Money Growth, Inflation, and the Nominal Interest Rate
   F. A Trend in the Real Demand for Money
   G. A shift in the Money Growth Rate
   H. Government Revenue form Printing Money

Teaching Tips:

1. This chapter covers a lot of ground, so it may require more class time than other chapters. If pressed for time, you could skip the section on measurement of expected inflation.

2. The "neutrality" of money is one of the key results of the equilibrium model. Remind students of this fact when examining the international data on monetary growth rates and inflation rates. If money is neutral, ask students why there should be such clear differences in monetary growth rates? Apart from the ability to raise government revenue, are there any advantages to inflation? (Hint: how do people feel about getting raises every year?)

3. One of the difficult concepts for students to use correctly is the idea of real money balances, but understanding how real money balances evolve is important to the results of the chapter. The "By the numbers" example on page 285 provides concrete examples that will help students apply the theory properly.

Answers to review questions, pg. 287

1. a. false. A constant rate of inflation will be incorporated into a constant nominal rate.

b. true. An growing rate of inflation will cause corresponding changes in i.

2. The real interest rate is the nominal interest rate – inflation. Positive rates of inflation change the purchasing power of money over time, reducing the real value of interest. Higher nominal rates are needed to compensate lenders for this loss in purchasing power.

3. The actual rate can only be determined after the fact, when actual inflation rates can be measured. Before the fact, inflation rates can only be predicted.

4. The Livingston survey is survey of 50 economists concerning inflation forecasts. The forecast uses "experts" as opposed to households. The extent to which household expectations relate to those of the experts is not known. Also, how do we determine whether the sample chosen is representative of the entire group? On the other hand, to the extent that decision makers are looking at these forecasts when formulating their own expectations, the survey is an economical way and reliable source of information.

5. The nominal rate cannot determine the opportunity cost of consuming goods today rather than in the future. Only the real interest rate can do that, because it takes into account changes in the future price of goods. The same argument applies to the labor supply decision, which is also based on the opportunity cost of current vs. future leisure.

Answers to Problems for Discussion, pg. 287-88

6. a. A high rate of growth in real GDP weakens the link between μ and π.. If the real economy grows at about the same rate as the money supply, there is no reason to expect positive rates of inflation. Given the assumptions on money demand made in this problem, money demand will grow at the same rate as the money supply.

b. A rising nominal interest rate reduces the growth in the real demand for money. For a given growth rate in the supply of money, this would result in a higher rate of inflation.

c. Higher rates of expected inflation leads to higher nominal interest rates, reducing the demand for money and creating inflationary pressure in the economy. The expectation of inflation can create the inflation.

7. a. The results are shown below (results were obtained using MS excel):

	Coefficients	*Standard Error*	*t Stat*
Intercept	0.037889295	0.006393448	5.926269
μ	0.054718207	0.081535388	0.671098

Interpretation: The predicted inflation rate is approximately 3.8% plus 0.055*change in the growth rate of currency (where the growth rate of the currency is expressed as a decimal).

b. The results are shown below:

	Coefficients	*Standard Error*	*t Stat*
Intercept	-0.00879	0.009138	-0.96185
$\Delta Y/Y$	1.006961	0.201987	4.985284

Interpretation: The growth rate in real balances is strongly related to the growth rate in real output. In particular, the intercept is near zero and the slope is approximately 1, which implies the growth rate in real balances is virtually equal to the growth rate in real output.

c. The results are shown below:

	Coefficients	*Standard Error*	*t Stat*
Intercept	0.03710586	0.006156435	6.027166
μ	0.19093438	0.120475626	1.584838
$\Delta Y/Y$	-0.22702226	0.152706513	-1.48666

Adding the growth rate of real GDP changes the results in part a. In this case, the base inflation rate doesn't change much, but the influence of monetary growth is much more significant (.19 compared to .055). This is offset by the coefficient on $\Delta Y/Y$ which has a negative sign. This implies that growth rates in real GDP reduce inflation rates (by about .23*change in the growth rate of real output).

8. a. the price level increases proportionately, but nominal interest rates do not change.

b. the increase in the money growth rate causes a similar increase in inflation and nominal interest rates. The price level "jumps" during the transition to a higher level.

c. prices increase because of the reduction in money demand, nominal interest rates rise.

9. a. The high demand for money would create a disequilibrium at the current price level; prices would tend to fall during periods of increased money demand

and rise after the first of the year. Short term inflation and nominal rates would follow the same pattern.

b. Temporary increases in the growth rate of money supply in the 4th quarter followed by slower first quarter increases would maintain equilibrium in the money markets.

10. If there is a temporary increase in money demand then people will want to increase their money balances. As we saw in chapter 10, this would cause a one time reduction in the price level. This does not affect nominal interest rates however, because the one time change in the price level has no effect on the growth rate of money. Therefore, by the equation $i=r+\pi$, the nominal interest rate will not change. However, if the central bank wanted to prevent even a one-time change in the price level, they would have to grow the nominal money supply temporarily, and then shrink it once the event is over. If the public recognizes the temporary nature of the increased money supply growth, then there will be no change in prices or interest rates. A credible announcement of its intentions will help calm inflationary fears. The FED attempted something very similar to this in the months leading up to the Y2K scare. They allowed the money supply to grow quickly before the year 1999 ended, and reduced the growth rate in the following period. If the increase in money demand is permanent, then the increase in money supply must also be permanent. Once again, there should be no effects on either prices or nominal interest rates figure 11.9. One way for the central bank to gain credibility is to announce a target for inflation. Countries that do this credibly have an essentially passive monetary policy that accommodates changes in money demand without causing inflation. The nominal interest rate changes only in response to changes in the real interest rate.

11. Government revenue from printing money increases with μ, but decreases with respect to real balances, (see equation 11.22 on page 284) Higher μ will lead to higher nominal rates, which reduce money demand. The more sensitive money demand is to these nominal rates, the more it will reduce the government's real revenue from printing money.

12. a. Issuers are likely to "call" the bond when the nominal rate on the bond is higher than the nominal rate on the market. A unexpected reduction in the nominal rate would trigger the increase in prepayments.

b. Nominal interest rates were rising during the initial period, falling thereafter. Prepayment works against the borrower when interest rates increase unexpectedly and in their favor when they fall.

c. The prepayment option becomes more valuable in an environment of volatile and unpredictable interest rates. The borrower can benefit from prepayment when the movement in interest rates is significantly lower than the rate on their original loan.

13. Rational expectations allows us to make use of all available information to identify the expected rate during the period in question. However, it is also difficult to determine the extent to which decision makers will actually attempt to gather and process this information. Sophisticated statistical models using data that is difficult to gather and interpret may help the forecaster formulate their own expectations, but won't necessarily explain how decision makers formulate their forecasts.

14. a. The nominal rate is 5%. The expected rate is 5%-the expected rate of inflation. The actual rate is 5%-the actual rate of inflation. Obviously the real rate depends on information which cannot be know until after the purchase.

b. In this case the actual real interest rate is 3%, and the actual nominal rate is 3% + π. The expected nominal rate is 3% + the predicted rate of inflation.

c. Answers may vary. One approach would be to peg the final interest payment to an average of short term interest rates + inflation over the term. Holders will be protected from the uncertainty associated with changes in both inflation rates and real interest rates in this case.

15. The counterfeiting was sufficient to create some inflation and higher nominal interest rates, which would ultimately lead to lower real money balances. By equation 11.22, we see that this would have reduced government's ability to increase revenue from the creation of money. In a sense, the competition hurt government's profits!

Chapter 12: Government Expenditure

Chapter Summary:

This unit, along with the next two chapters, challenges much of the conventional wisdom about the economic effects of expansionary fiscal policy. The chapter begins by describing the components of government spending, making a distinction between government expenditures and transfers. Historical data from the U.S. is presented, and international comparisons. Afterward, the theory is developed by the links between two budget constraints: that of the government, and that of the household. The link between these two budget constraints shows how changes in spending policy affect household behavior. In particular, temporary changes are found to have potentially large negative impact on investment, while permanent changes are found to have a negative impact on consumption. This is in keeping with the intertemporal nature of the household budget constraint. Neither change is found to have an impact on real GDP. However, in at least one important case, the empirical evidence seems to contradict this result. This is the case of wartime spending, which is correlated with large increases in real GDP. The explanation offered here shows that supply side factors may account for this apparent anomaly.

Chapter Outline:

I. Data on Government Expenditure

II. The Government's Budget Constraint

III. Public Production

IV. Public Services

V. The Household's Budget Constraint

VI. Permanent Changes in Government Purchases
   A. A Permanent Change in Government Purchases: Theory
   B. The Cyclical Behavior of Government Purchases

VII. Temporary Changes in Government Purchases
   A. A Temporary Change in Government Purchases: Theory
   B. Wartime Effects on the Economy
      i. Employment during wartime
      ii. Effects of war on labor supply
      iii. Effects of war on the real wage rate
      iv. Effects of war on the rental market

Teaching Tips:

1. Students are likely to question the conclusions of the model regarding the neutrality of permanent government spending on real GDP, real interest rates, real wage rates, and most importantly, on the level of investment. Help them to draw a parallel with the neutrality of money example found in chapter 10. Reinforce the fact that in the equilibrium business cycle model, the supply of labor and capital is essential fixed, markets are assumed to clear. If a new government program fails to change either the supply or productivity of capital and labor services, aggregate real GDP will not change.

2. When discussing equations (12.3) and (12.4), it may be helpful to review figure 7.1 on page 151 and demonstrate how the budget constraint reacts to various changes in fiscal policy. How does it respond to current and future changes in V and T?

3. The discussion of the effects of wartime spending is particularly timely, considering the conflict in Iraq. Prior to assigning the reading, solicit student opinions about the economic impact of the spending on the "war on terror". Then ask them to read the empirical evidence beginning on page 308.

4. The rather dry discussion on page 305 concerning the efficacy of government spending compared to private spending does not convey the depth of passion people feel about "big government". The late Milton Friedman often asserted that "No one spends another person's money as carefully as he spends his own." Barro was once challenged by Friedman to "name one government program" that provided net benefits in excess of its opportunity costs. Barro replied, "national defense", to which Friedman responded, "name another". Certainly the characteristics of national defense make help to explain Friedman's reaction: it is a non-rival and non-excludable good. This exchange can help students develop more precise criteria by which to evaluate the role of government spending. Use Friedman's question to challenge your students and see if they come up with similar responses.

Answers to review questions, pg. 316

1. Transfer payments do not make any claim on GDP but government purchases do. Both transfers and purchases must be financed as indicated by the government budget constraint (in our model, this requires money creation or taxation- later we will consider a third alternative-borrowing.) From the perspective of the consumer, transfers are treated as a source of income which can be spent on utility increasing goods. To the extent that government purchases are useful, these may also be perceived by the consumer as contributing to utility. If the government understands consumer preferences, is efficient in its procurement process, and can identify goods and services where there are economies of scale or positive externalities associated with the purchase, then government purchases could provide more utility than what can be obtained through private purchases. It all depends on the value of λ (see boxed example on page 305).

2. For a detailed description refer to the derivation of the multi-year budget constraint on pages 170-171. Only in this case we rewrite eq. 7.9 to include the effects of taxes and transfers and substitute the real interest rate for the nominal rate (recall the assumption that inflation = zero) to get: $C_1+C_2/(1+r_1)=(1+r_0)(B_0/P+K_0)+(w/P)_1*L+(w/P_2)*L/(1+r_1)-(B_2/P+K_2)/(1+r_1)+(V_1-T_1)+(V_2-T_2)/(1+r_1)$. From there we can follow the procedure outlined in the appendix to chapter 7.

Answers to problems for discussion, pg. 316-317

3. a. If public and private security guards are perfect substitutes in production, there should be no impact on GDP. However, because national income accounts treat government purchases of labor as a final good, the measured GDP will increase. This is a case of "double counting".

b. Various answers are possible, but the obvious one would be to classify government purchases according to whether they are used to purchase inputs or outputs of the production process. Such a classification system would be far from objective. For example, if an employer provides a free lunch for its employees it is treated as an input to the production process, just as much as the labor itself. When the individual buys their lunch at a restaurant, it is treated as a final good. Consider education, health care, and a variety of other services, and the same ambiguity appears.

4. a. Prior to the 1996 revisions, the services provided by the capital would have added nothing to GDP. If they were given to the private sector and purchased by the government, GDP would increase. For example if government built a marina for coast guard patrol boats, the services would not be counted as GDP. If the government gave the dock to a private owner and paid the private owner rental fees, the GDP would increase.

b. Under government ownership the implicit flow of services would be valued at the estimated depreciation rate of the dock. If they gave it to a private owner and rented it, then the GDP would increase by that amount. In this case, since the market value of the service is likely to be greater than the estimated depreciation rate, government ownership is still likely to understate the true GDP, though the bias will be reduced.

5. a. Based on the assumptions of the model used in this chapter, we will treat the government purchase as a reduction in future income (λ=0). If the capital and labor supply is fixed, there will be no change in GDP. Because of consumption smoothing, people will reduce current consumption, and investment will increase. This could occur during election years when the leading candidate is proposing a significant expansion of government programs.

6. The explanation provided in the question leads one to believe that business may have raised prices in anticipation of price controls being imposed. We can also observe that the growth rate in the money supply did increase during the war. We saw in chapter 11 that an increase in the growth rate of the money supply can cause an upward jump in the price level (see fig. 11.9) due to the reduction in money demand associated with higher inflation rates.

7. When the actual benefits of a policy are difficult to measure, as in the case of military spending or environmental conservation, it may be difficult to establish a consensus regarding the efficiency of government purchases. To the extent that these decisions are determined by special interest groups, the costs may be widely dispersed and the benefits highly concentrated. The theory of public choice suggest that those who bear the cost will not base their vote on that issue, but those who benefit may very well do so. (For example, politicians may support a weapons program the pentagon doesn't want or need, because it contributes to the economy of their home district.) To the extent that the costs are spread out and the benefits are concentrated, we can expect many government purchases to provide negative net benefits. On the other hand, to the

extent that the people who bear the cost of a government program are also the ones who benefit, it is more likely that programs providing negative net benefits will be rejected. Local decisions regarding the level of fire protection, education, and other public goods are likely to be more efficient because they are largely provided with local taxes on the residents who receive the primary benefit.

Chapter 13: Taxes

Chapter Summary:

This chapter focuses on the incentive effects of taxation on both demand and supply side variables. It begins with a brief historical review of U.S. tax revenue by source for both federal and local units of government. It then examines how the burden of the income tax is divided among various income groups. One of the striking features of the data is the trend in the share of the income tax burden paid by the upper 50% of households; which account for nearly all of the revenue from the personal income tax.

The chapter then describes the impact of taxes on labor (reduced employment and real GDP and falling rental rates for capital). The tax on assets is shown to have a negative impact on capital accumulation and growth rates of real output. However the increase in government purchases can have income effects which increase labor supply, so the net impact on employment may be reduced. The **marginal tax rates** on factors of production are shown to have a negative effect on the size of the tax base. The net effect of the tax rate on revenue may be positive or negative, as indicated by the **Laffer curve**. Similar incentive effects are associated with means-tested transfer payments.

Chapter Outline:

I. Taxes in the United States

II. Types of Taxes

III. Taxes in the Model

A. A Tax on Labor Income

B. A Tax on Asset Income

IV. Transfer Payments

Teaching Tips:

1. For an empirical study of the optimal design of marginal tax rates, see Gruber and Saez at NBER: http://www.nber.org/digest/jul00/w7512.html. They recommend a tax which is progressive on average but should be regressive in the marginal tax rate. For a spirited debate on the topic, read the exchange between Robert Frank and Greg Mankiw at Mankiw's blogsite here: http://gregmankiw.blogspot.com/2007/04/bob-frank-replies.html

2. One of the objectives of this chapter is to demonstrate the substitution and income effects of marginal tax rates may have opposite effects on labor supply. This point should be emphasized. Although the chapter assumes that the income effects are minimal, the question can really only be solved by empirical research.

3. A system of low, flat marginal tax rates seems to be catching on in the former communist block, beginning with Russia's 13 % rate on personal income. This presents the question, if the U.S. were to start from scratch, would we design our tax code the way it is now? If not, why don't we change it? Students should be encouraged to think about the transition costs of changing tax systems, and how that might influence the politics of tax reform.

4. One of the frequent tax cuts provided periodically by the Federal government is the investment tax credit. The temporary nature of these tax credits creates the possibility that businesses will time their investments to coincide with the tax policy, creating a "lumpy" path for policy. Use this example to discuss the benefits of a predictable and stable tax policy.

Answers to review questions, pg. 338

1. The average tax rate is the *total* tax liability/*total* income, but the marginal tax rate is the *change* in tax liability/*change* in income. In the case of a flat tax that is incurred from the very first dollar of income, they would be equal. If there is a portion of income which is exempt from taxation, then the average tax rate will be lower than the marginal rate. In this case, the average rate will increase as income grows, but it will never "catch up" to the marginal rate.

2 Theoretically, if the labor supply is sufficiently elastic, the reduction in labor supplied would reduce the tax "base" so that total taxes collected decrease. This would require that the substitution effect would be much stronger than the income effects of the tax. This is more plausible when the marginal rates of taxation are extremely high to begin with.

3. Lower rates of consumption and leisure is a rational response to lower levels of income. Less leisure implies an increase in the labor supply. In the chapter it was assumed that the taxes would be used either to increase transfers or reduce other forms of taxation. That is, we assumed that G was fixed, (V-T) is unchanged. In this case, there would be no income effect because the household budget constraint would not change.

Answers to problems for discussion, pg. 338-339

4. a. If the elimination of deductions permits government to reduce the marginal tax rate on labor income, then the substitution effect predicts an increase in labor income. More labor employed will make capital more productive and should result in an increase in capacity utilization rates. The net result would be to raise GDP,Y.

   b. There are similarities. Currently, the payroll tax provides a constant marginal tax rate on labor income, just as the proposed flat tax would. However, social security taxes provide no exemption until income exceeds a particular level (approximately $90,000), after which the marginal tax rate falls to zero. Under this system, the average tax rate falls as incomes exceed the $90,000 mark. Under a flat tax, the exemption is applied to the first portion of earned income, so that the average rate increases with income. In other words, the social security tax is regressive in the average tax rate, but the flat tax is progressive.

5. a. The tax on consumption will raise the effective price; it will now take $(1+\tau_c)$ to purchase consumer goods. The household budget constraint can be written as:

$$(1+\tau_c)C+(1/P)\Delta B+\Delta K=(w/P)L^s+r(B/P+K)+V-T$$

   b. The tax on consumption reduces the effective opportunity cost of leisure in terms of current (and future) consumer goods. The labor supply would decrease by the substitution effect.

   c. The reduction in the labor supply found in part b would reduce the marginal product of capital services, just as in the earlier case. Capacity utilization rates and real interest rates would fall.

   d. This change introduces intertemporal substitution effects. Current consumption is less expensive than future consumption, so current consumption increases and real savings decreases. A tax on asset income would have a similar effect on real savings, because it would reduce the opportunity cost of current consumption.

6. I found the 2004 report contained more details than the 2005 report. The essential features of the 2001 package included reductions in marginal tax rates and the increase in child care tax credits, while in 2003 the tax cuts on income

from capital gains, accelerated allowances for depreciation, and investment tax credits appeared to be targeted toward reducing the cost of capital. The tax cuts reduce the cost of capital and raise the opportunity cost of current consumption. The prediction is that they would increase the rate of savings and investment, and labor supply. The "lump-sum" tax cuts such as the child care credit are not related to productive effort. The administration feels that the tax cuts contributed to the strength of the recovery and the increase in productivity, as seen in the following quote: "The tax cuts provided by this administration provided a substantial short-term stimulus to consumption and investment and promoted strong and sustainable long term growth." (pg.45 of the 2004 Economic Report to the President).

7. a. The increase in nominal wage and interest rates would have pushed individuals into brackets with higher marginal tax rates.

b. The indexing should maintain the "real income" tax brackets at their original levels; only changes in real income will cause a change in marginal tax rates.

8. a. Since $r=i-\pi$, after tax real rate of return is $(1-\tau_r)*i-\pi$. For example, if the tax rate is 20%, the nominal interest rate is 10% and inflation is 5%, then the after tax real rate of return is 3% =(.2*.1-.05).

b. The inflation rate will increase. Because of the impact on money demand, the price level will "jump" in the current period and will settle at a higher rate afterward, as in the graph on page 281.

c. Assuming that the tax applies to the real returns on capital, there will be no change in the after tax real return (recall that real interest rates are not affected by changes in μ.)

d. Because the money growth was unanticipated, the nominal interest rate will initially be too low to make up for the effects of the inflation. Bond holders will suffer the double indignity of suffering from unusually high inflation which reduces real returns, and then taxes which reduce them further. For example, if the expected rate of inflation was 2%, and the tax rate is 20%, then the after tax real return on nominal interest rate of 5% is expected to be 2%. If prices jump by 5%, then the after tax return is -1%. They end up paying taxes on their economic losses! In the future, as the nominal interest rate adjusts to the new higher rates of inflation by a multiple of (1+◎r) in order to maintain a particular after tax real rate of return.

9. a. Food stamps reduce the opportunity cost of leisure: labor supply decreases.

b. The EITC increases the opportunity cost of leisure for those with little earning power. The substitution effect on labor supply is positive. On the other hand, there are income effects associated with the transfer that would reduce labor supply. The net effects are ambiguous, although it is plausible to assume that the substitution effect would dominate at lower levels of income.

c. The opportunity cost of leisure is reduced for the period of eligibility; there is less labor supplied in both countries, but especially in Europe.

d. This policy is similar to a tax on wages, with similar effects on labor supply. The substitution effect reduces labor supplied by this particular group of workers.

Chapter 14: Public Debt

Chapter Summary:

A look at the U.S. and U.K. debt ratios provides a historical perspective for evaluating the government and deficits. Students should note that the debt to GDP ratio tends to peak during wartime and recedes afterward. The government budget constraint introduced in chapter 12 is augmented to include real interest payments and the change in real debt. The concept of **Ricardian Equivalence** that government saving and household saving are substitutes; students should recognize that government bonds impose a future tax burden that is equal (in present value terms) to the current deficit. Therefore, the impact of the deficit on household budget constraint is no different from a balanced budget. The result is that deficits do not change the intertemporal pattern of spending in the economy. Tax cuts may have real effects on GDP if they alter the timing of household's decisions; if the tax is imposed on income from labor and capital, changes in the tax rate will create intertemporal substitution effects on labor supply and investment. These intertemporal distortions can be avoided by **tax-rate smoothing**- maintaining fairly stable tax rates over time.

One of the conclusions of this chapter is that deficit financing is not particularly important; however, the government spending which it finances is important. Government spending imposes opportunity costs on society whether it is financed by issuing debt, raising taxes, or even **open market operations** (see the "Back to Reality section on page 359). The tendency in recent decades for government spending to grow over time has given rise to the possibility of **strategic deficits** - deficits which create public concern over government finances and create public pressure to limit the growth of government programs. The Reagan deficits of the 1980's may have been motivated by these concerns.

The standard view of a budget deficit, in which Ricardian equivalence fails, is that increasing government debt leads to higher interest rates and lower levels of investment. One possible reason for Ricardian equivalence to fail is that the lifetimes of the current generation of taxpayers is finite, which implies they may be able to impose the future taxes on to another generation of taxpayers. In this case, a tax cut will be treated as an increase in their wealth. This may be offset somewhat by their desire to leave bequests to the next generation. Another reason is imperfections in credit markets. In this case the interest rate on private borrowing will be higher than the government rate, a tax cut will increase their wealth because it reduces the present value of their debt. In this case, the deficits have a beneficial effect on the economy by allocating credit more efficiently.

No discussion of the debt should ignore the impact of the promises made under the social security program, which represents a huge financial commitment that dwarfs the official debt. The treatment of this debt is similar to the government issue of bonds; if Ricardian equivalence holds, there should be no significant macroeconomic effects; if not, then national savings rates will fall along with investment and economic growth. The **finite lifetimes** problem discussed earlier may apply in this case.

Chapter Outline:

I. The History of U.S. and U.K. Public Debt

II. Characteristics of Government Bonds

III. Budget Constraints and Budget Deficits
- A. The Government's Budget Constraint
- B. The Budget Deficit
- C. Public Saving, Private Saving, and National Saving
- D. A Simple Case of Ricardian Equivalence
- E. Another Case of Ricardian Equivalence
- F. Ricardian Equivalence More Generally

IV. Economic Effects of a Budget Deficit
- A. Lump-sum Taxes
- A. Labor Income Taxes
- B. Asset Income Taxes
- C. The timing of Taxes and Tax-Rate Smoothing
- D. Strategic Budget Deficits
- E. The Standard View of a Budget Deficit
  - i. Finite lifetimes
  - ii. Imperfect credit markets

V. Social Security

VI. Open-Market Operations

Teaching Tips:

1. The students may or may not know that Barro is a columnist who writes for the popular press. After encountering his entertaining and informative columns in BusinessWeek, they may have a new appreciation for his writing ability. His columns on fiscal policy are particularly good conversation starters. His column "It's The Spending Stupid, Not the Deficit" (March 1, 2004) is a good example of the difference between positive economics of the type found in his textbook, and normative economics of the type found in his columns. Many of the concepts presented formally in this chapter are presented for a popular audience in this column.

2. A two period intertemporal budget constraint is a useful visual tool for showing Ricardian equivalence. For example, in the graph shown here, government spends $100 on "foreign aid", so that the income of the tax payer falls by 100 now (if taxes increase now) or 110 next period(the interest rate used here is 10%). Because either scenario puts them on the same budget line, there is no difference in their intertemporal pattern of consumption. They will simply adjust their private savings to achieve the pattern of consumption they prefer.

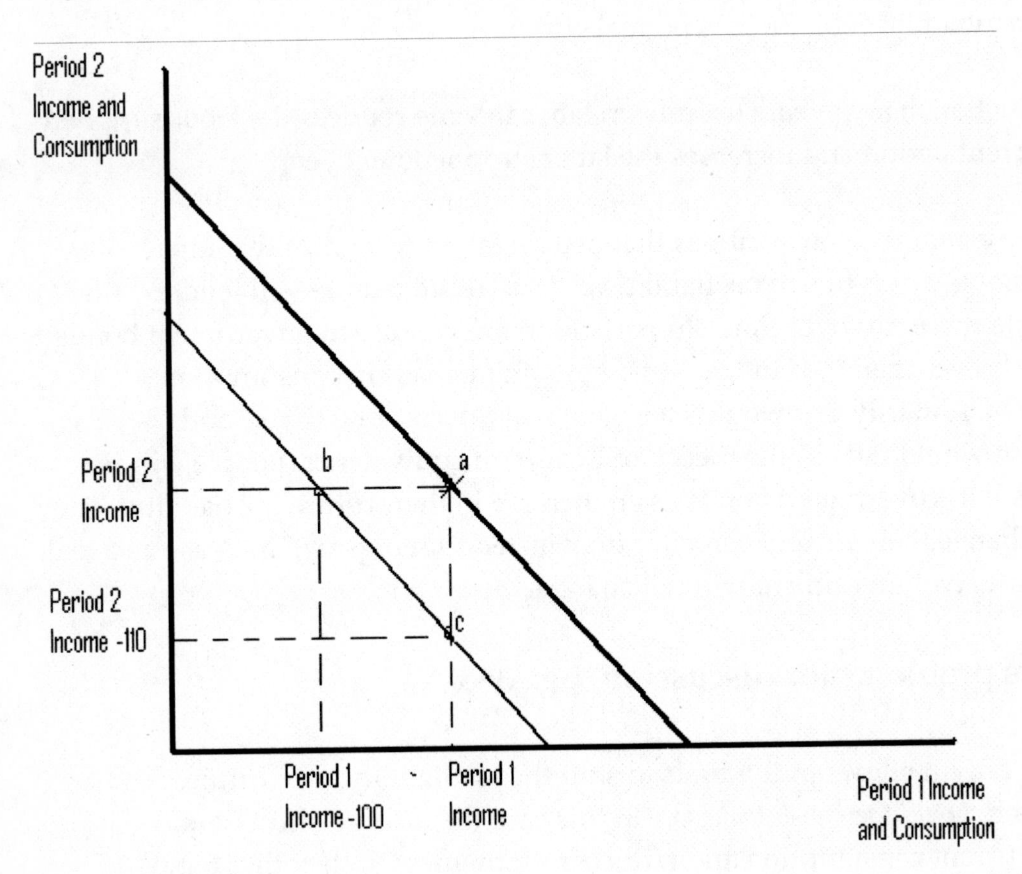

3. The way in which imperfection of credit markets can be used to make a case in favor of increasing government deficits can be vividly illustrated with the example of the Great Depression. Because the period was a temporary reduction in income, the logic of consumption smoothing would have indicated a great need for private credit to expand. Instead, credit markets dried up. A flight to quality meant that the interest rates on government debt were much lower than on private debt. Unfortunately, Hoover and Roosevelt both raised taxes during the depression in an attempt to balance the budget, violating the "tax smoothing" policies recommended in the chapter. The model suggests that the tax increases made people worse off.

Answers to review questions, pg. 368

1. Open market operations are purchases of government bonds by the central bank. The creation of money used to purchase the bonds can be compared to two separate policies: a policy of a one-time increase in the money supply and a reduction in public debt. The increase in the money supply will cause prices to rise, but will have no real effects. If Ricardian equivalence holds then the reduction in public debt also has no real effects.

2. A reduction in next years tax rate on labor income reduces the labor supplied in the current period and increases the labor supplied next year.

3. The conventional view assumes that people fail to recognize the impact of current tax policy on future tax liabilities. As a result, people will tend to misallocate resources over time. In particular, an increase in government bonds will allow government to cut taxes and spur an increase in consumption spending. Ordinarily this would cause the real interest rate to rise and investment would fall. In the theory of Ricardian equivalence, people will see the increase in government bonds as an increase in their future tax liability. They will not change their current consumption, instead savings will increase and real interest rates and investment will not change.

Answers problems for discussion, pg. 368

4. a. The tax cut allows individuals to shift the tax liability onto future generations *should they wish to do so.* In this case the income effect would increase current consumption and reduce investment. On the other hand, if people care about the the finances of the next generation, they will accumulate

savings which will be left to their children (bequest motive) and the income effects will be eliminated.

b. If people don't have any children then they will be able to shift the burden of the debt onto other people's children. The bequest motive is weakened, and the income effect is larger than in the previous example.

c. Just as in case b, people may feel that "someone else" will be liable for the future taxes. In this case, a positive income effect is likely.

d. The increase in the stock of money will create inflation, which is a kind of tax. Therefore there is no change in the present value of household income and no income effect.

5. The phased-in income tax cuts changed the after tax real wage rate and generated intertemporal substitution effects on the labor supply. In particular, there would be an incentive to increase leisure in the initial phase and reduce it in later phases. This would create a path for GDP in which it would grow below trend initially and above trend toward the end of the period.

6. a. The capital stock will fall if people view the government program as an increase in current taxes to be offset by a corresponding increase in future transfers. The reduction in current after tax income will be offset by an increase in future after tax income. If the present value of benefits is just equal to the present value of taxes, then people would simply use the credit markets to achieve their desired pattern of consumption over their lifetimes. However, if the present value of expected benefits is higher than current taxes, then there will be an increase in current consumption. This implies a reduction in savings during the initial period which would decrease the rate of capital accumulation.

b. In a pay as you go system, your savings do not determine your retirement benefit. An increase in current benefits can be achieved by raising taxes on the current generation of workers. Therefore, it is possible to generate the income effects seen in part a- but *only if the bequest motive is weak.* If current beneficiaries are concerned about the effect of the current policy on future generations, they could leave larger bequests. On the other hand, the trust fund would clearly eliminate any uncertainty of the matter, since it would be impossible to increase benefits by imposing larger tax burdens on the current generation. Benefits would have to come from the accumulated balance of the trust fund, which is determined by past taxes collected.

Chapter 15: Money and Business Cycles I: The Price-Misperceptions Model.

Chapter Summary:

This is the first of two chapters which use the framework of the equilibrium business cycle model to demonstrate how monetary shocks could create business cycles. The conditions under which this could happen are implicit in the chapter titles themselves; in this case "price misperceptions" and in the next chapter "sticky prices and wages".

Students are shown that the historical evidence suggests that although money is neutral over lengthy time periods, it appears as though it does have important short term effects. The work of Freidman and Schwartz is particularly influential in this regard, demonstrating that exogenous fluctuations in the money supply have occurred regularly and appear to have caused similar fluctuations in real GDP. The mechanism used in this chapter to explain this observation is the idea of monetary misperceptions in the labor market. In particular, workers are assumed to have imperfect information about the price level. In this case, unanticipated increases in the money supply cause workers to overestimate the real wage offers during the period, and the labor supply curve shifts to the right as a result. Two of the major results of the model is that real wages are countercyclical, and prices are procyclical. This contradicts the predictions of the equilibrium business cycle model discussed in previous chapters. In cases where the cycle is caused by technological shocks, the monetary misperceptions model indicates that the real effects of these shocks will be somewhat smaller than indicated in chapter 8.

The results depend on monetary policy catching workers by surprise. The **Lucas hypothesis** suggests that this may be more difficult in countries which normally have high and variable rates of inflation. Paradoxically, countries which rely heavily on monetary policy to influence the economy are less able to do so than countries that have historically chosen monetary restraint.

The policy implications for dealing with the model are discussed at length. **Discretion** in monetary policy is analyzed using a game-theoretic framework in which the policymaker's choice of inflation is chosen on the basis of the public's expected rate of inflation. In this case, the desirability of raising inflation above expected levels decreases as inflationary expectations rise. Alternatively, rules for guiding monetary policy are considered as a way to minimize the potential for monetary "surprises" and the short run shocks they can create. Several rules are considered, including the monetary growth rule, targeting nominal GDP, and targeting the inflation rate. An explicit inflation rate targets may increase the central bank's credibility and transparency which would allow them to reduce inflation rates with causing temporary reductions in real GDP. The current trend of countries to move to an explicit inflation rate target is discussed.

I. Effects of Money in the Equilibrium Business-Cycle Model

II. The Price-Misperceptions Model
   A. A Model with Non-Neutral Effects of Money
   B. Money Is Neutral in the Long Run
   C. Only Unperceived Inflation Affects Real Variables
   D. Predictions for Economic Fluctuations
   E. Empirical Evidence on the Real Effects of Monetary Shocks
      i. Friedman and Schwartz's Monetary History of the U.S.
      ii. Unanticipated money growth
      iii. Romer and Romer on Federal Reserve policy
   F. Real Shocks

III. Rules Versus Discretion

Teaching Tips:

1. The students should be encouraged to think of the rules vs. discretion debate as an exciting theoretical debate with real policy relevance. The difficulty of timing discretionary policy correctly is illustrated in a brief Wall Street Journal article titled "Fed Debate on 2000 Tech Bust Holds Lesson on Current Risks" from the April 5, 2006 edition. For those with online access to the WSJ, it is found here:
http://online.wsj.com/article/SB114416283640416562.html
The article shows that the FOMC continued to maintain a relatively high target for the Fed Funds rate of 6.5% even as investment spending had "screeched to halt" in the second half of 2000. It was not until the beginning of 2001 that the Fed began to reduce its interest rate targets.

2. Although the basic concept of labor supply responding to inaccurate estimates of the price level is a simple one, the behavior of individuals may be harder for students to grasp. After all, individual job seekers are not necessarily well informed enough to even consider price level movements when evaluating job offers. The process by which reservation wages are formed is not as rational as

the model seems to indicate. It is not necessary to fully understand how reservation wages are formed however, to generate the results of the model. It is enough to know that once reservation wages have been formed, an increase in the price level will generate more job offers available at any given nominal wage, and the duration of job searches will be reduced. This is enough to generate the shift in the labor supply curve shown in figure 15.2.

3. The analysis of optimal monetary policy using concepts from game theory is an important feature of the model. For students unfamiliar with game theory, the game "rock, paper, scissors" can be used to illustrate the nature of the game played by economic agents and the central bank. If the only way that the central bank can "win" is by surprising the public, then the only effective policy will be one that is inherently unpredictable. But the **Lucas hypothesis** casts doubt on whether such a strategy exists.

4. The discussion of figure 15.4 is important, but difficult for students to intuitively understand. Therefore, sufficient time and concrete examples should be used to explain the determinants of the red curve. Questions such as "why is the vertical intercept positive?" and "why is the slope less than one?" should help students process the information depicted in the graph.

Answers to review questions, pg. 388

1. Obtaining information is an economic activity; it generates marginal benefits and marginal costs. Some of these costs include time, subscriptions to relevant data, investment in human capital necessary to process the data (like this economics class!) and others. The rational choice is not to obtain the most accurate estimate possible. Instead, rational people will pursue accuracy up to the point where marginal benefits are equal to the marginal costs.

2. A relative price is the opportunity cost of one good expressed in terms of the other. For example, if bananas cost $1 and dates cost $4, the relative price of dates is 4 (4 bananas per date). The real wage is a relative price that defines the real terms of trade between leisure and other goods in the economy. For example, if w=10 and P=$2, then the relative price of leisure is 5; (5 goods per unit of leisure enjoyed)

3. Rational expectations does not imply that people are always right. What it implies is that people will generate unbiased forecasts based on available

information. Unanticipated "shocks" are not foreseeable; however, if these "shocks" produce random errors then an unbiased forecast is possible. Whether or not a policy maker can produce a "surprise" more than once is debatable; the Lucas hypothesis suggests that the real effects of a monetary shock are smaller in countries that have a history of less predictable monetary growth rates.

4. Workers may suffer from "money illusion" if they fail to anticipate changes in the price level as they occur. This is more likely to be the case if the central bank breaks away from historical patterns. If the change in monetary policy is announced in advance, then this will help alert workers only if the central bank has credibility.

Answers to Problems for discussion, pg. 388-389

5. The model predicts that deviations from trend GDP will be temporary. Persistent effects on GDP can arise from other sources. For example, a shock that produces above trend GDP will generate an increase in income, some of which will be devoted to investment. The investment will raise the capital stock and increase future labor productivity, The result is a persistent increase in employment and output, even though labor supply curve has shifted back to its original position.

6. Correlation is not causation. It could be that the central bank is forecasting economic activity accurately, and adjusting the money supply to keep up with anticipated changes in money demand (recall that money demand increases as GDP increases). Even if the central bank does not actively manage the money supply, M1 would still increase prior to an investment boom because bank lending expands the volume of demand deposits. An investment boom could be associated with a technological change that increases productivity. In this case, the expansion in the money supply "accommodates" the expansion of real GDP rather than causing it.

7. a. If people accurately anticipate the effects of monetary policy on inflation, and assuming there are no impediments to changing nominal prices, then nominal prices will adjust to maintain real wages, real rental rates for capital services, real interest rates, etc. If regulations, "menu costs", long term contracts, or other impediments to price flexibility exist, then the monetary policy will have real effects.

b. In a system of completely flexible prices, only unanticipated changes in monetary policy are likely to generate real effects.

c. The results of part a can be applied to a number of other government policies. For example, in case (i) the tax cuts can be incorporated into the household's multi-period budget constraint. In this case, the household, because of consumption smoothing, the tax cut will not change spending patterns. A similar argument can be made for the other two examples.

Chapter 16: Money and Business Cycles II: Sticky Prices and Nominal Wage Rates

Chapter Summary:

The original Keynesian model of recession and unemployment was based on "**sticky wages**". This produced countercyclical movements in the real wage and procyclical movements in the price level, just as the monetary misperceptions model. Empirical evidence since 1950 has not supported that idea, and economists working in the Keynesian tradition developed a "**sticky price**" model that predicts a procyclical real wage. Although the chapter reviews the sticky wage theory, the major focus is on the sticky price model. The key assumption of the theory is that of **imperfect competition** in which firms establish prices using the **markup ratio**. This markup ratio is flexible; it provides firms with "wiggle room" to choose their own price, and they may respond to changes in demand by expanding output. This in turn increases the demand for labor, and produces a procyclical pattern in employment and real wage rates. However, since these changes are the result of shifts in the labor demand, the increase in employment reduced the average product of labor, contrary to empirical evidence. A theory of **labor hoarding** may be used to explain this apparent weakness in the model.

In this theory, open-market operations produce real effects on the economy, and the central bank conducts monetary policy in order to influence nominal interest rates and aggregate demand. The discussion of Federal Reserve policy beginning on page 401 demonstrates how economic theory impacts "real world" policies. Students should see that experience of the last few decades has produced important changes in the way the Federal Reserve conducts monetary policy.

Chapter Outline:

I. The New Keynesian Model
   - A. Price Setting Under Imperfect Competition
   - B. Short-Rum Responses to a Monetary Shock
   - C. New Keynesian Predictions
   - D. Price Adjustment in the Long run
   - E. Comparing Predication for Economic Fluctuation
   - F. Shocks to Aggregate Demand

II. Money and Nominal Interest Rates

II. The Keynesian Model-Sticky Nominal Wage Rates

III. Long-Term Contracts and Sticky Nominal Wage Rates

Teaching Tips:

1. The Great Depression was the key event in the development of modern macroeconomics. Students should be encouraged to think about the development of economic that results from historical experience. The "back to reality" should be presented. Unfortunately students may perceive, incorrectly, that business cycle theory began with Keynes. However, business cycle theory was an important part of the "Austrian" school led by Mises and Hayek prior to the publication of Keynes' "General Theory". The rising tide of Keynesian thought eclipsed the Austrian view, but they have been gaining more adherents in recent years. The Economist magazine has an article describing the resurgence of the Austrian School entitled, "A Necessary Evil" on page 18 of the Sept. 28, 2002 issue.

2. Prior to his being appointed to serve as the Chairman of the Federal Reserve Board, Ben Bernanke advocated an approach he called "constrained discretion." Here is his definition of that approach:

" The approach to monetary policy that I call constrained discretion can be defined by two simple and parsimonious principles.

First, through its words and (especially) its actions, *the central bank must establish a strong commitment to keeping inflation low and stable.*

Second, *subject to the condition that inflation be kept low and stable,* and to the extent possible given our uncertainties about the structure of the economy and the effects of policy, *monetary policy should strive to limit cyclical swings in resource utilization."*

The rest of this speech can be found here:
http://www.federalreserve.gov/boarddocs/speeches/2003/20030203/

3. Table 16.1, showing the differences in the predictions of the various models should be reviewed carefully, and the root causes of these differences reviewed as well.

Answers to review questions, pg. 412

1. Involuntary unemployment occurs when qualified job seekers are willing to work at the market wage rate, but cannot do so because of the lack of job offers. In the flexible price model, involuntary unemployment is eliminated by a falling real wage, but in the sticky nominal wage model discussed here, the real wage does not clear the market.

2. For a given level of money demand, an increase in the supply of money will create a disequilibrium in the money market; people will have higher money balances than they wish to hold. In that case, people will seek to adjust their portfolios by purchasing more bonds (among other things), causing the bond prices to rise and nominal interest rates to fall. In the U.S., the money supply would increase when the Federal Reserve Banking System engages in open market operations, using bond purchases to inject money into the economy. This leads to higher bond prices and lower nominal rates. In a world of flexible prices, these higher nominal rates would be offset to a certain extent by an increase in inflation rates, but in this case, the assumption of "sticky prices" prevents that from happening.

B. Problems for discussion, pg. 412-413

3. a. The new Keynesian model assumes that prices and nominal wages are slow to respond to changes in market conditions; and that technology is fixed, and it is shocks in aggregate demand rather than supply which cause cyclical fluctuations in GDP.

b. In the new Keynesian model, a change in M has real effects on the economy. Increases in the money supply lead to increases in aggregate demand which translate into increases in real output. Imperfect competition among producers is *not sufficient* to guarantee this result; after all, firms could raise prices and wages in response to the increase in the money supply, leaving both the real wage rate and the ratio of each firm's price to the average price unchanged. However, the imperfect competition assumption *is necessary* in the the sense that it gives firms some "wiggle-room" to raise real wages. In this case, the additional demand can be filled by an increase in employment and output without imposing economic losses on the firms.

c. There are two explanations provided in the text- imperfect competition and menu costs.

d. The model with sticky prices generates a pro cyclical real wage rate, which is consistent with the empirical evidence. However, its assumption that technology is unchanged implies that more labor employed reduces the marginal and average product of labor, a prediction which is refuted by the empirical evidence.

e. Money-supply shocks are not the only source of shocks in the model: any unanticipated change in demand can have a similar impact. This could arise from an unexpected change in consumer behavior (a reduction in the savings rate for example) or fiscal policy (government spending or tax cuts, for example), and foreign trade (an increase in net exports due to the prosperity of a trading partner, for example), and other sources.

f. The new Keynesian model represents an advance over the old in the sense that it incorporates more micro-economic foundations and is consistent with much of the empirical evidence of business cycles. The exception is the countercyclical prediction for the average product of labor, although the theory of labor hoarding may account for this. It explains why changes in the money supply can have real effects on output and employment even when those changes are anticipated. The strength of the equilibrium business cycle model is its ability to account for all the relationships in terms of technological, or supply side "shocks" in a way that is consistent with the empirical evidence. The problem with it is that it cannot explain why changes in the money supply would have any real effects on the economy.

4. a. The reduction in aggregate demand reduces real output and employment.

b. In the one hand savings will increase relative to consumption, due to the higher savings rate. Although it is theoretically possible that savings could fall in the aggregate, this would require that real GDP falls by a multiple of the original change in consumption. If real wages and employment fall, then spending could drop further than originally planned, leading to further reductions in income and spending. The end result could be the *paradox of thrift* described in the chapter.

c. Because the equilibrium business cycle model is based on supply side factors, the idea that an increase in savings would lead to a reduction in real output doesn't apply. In this case, the increase in savings would simply result in higher rates of investment. Therefore, there is no multiple reduction in spending and income as in the Keynesian model.

5. The multiplier is based on the assumption that initial changes in demand reduce real output rather than prices. The reduction in real output results in low levels of spending, generating additional reductions in real output, and so on.
5a. If the price level adjusts, then the change in nominal spending will not have as much effect on real output; the multiplier is reduced.
5b. The markup ratio provides the "wiggle room" that firms have to raise real wages without compromising profitability. The less "wiggle room" firms have, the more pressure there will be to raise prices. Therefore the multiplier would increase with the size of the markup ratio.

5c. The model assumes that people will attempt to exchange their excess money balances for goods. If the demand for real money balances grows along with GDP, Y, then people will not have excess money balances and the multiplier effect is reduced. In an extreme case, referred to as a "liquidity trap" by Keynes, the money demand will grow to accommodate any increase in the money supplied. In this case, he felt that monetary policy could not be relied upon to generate the necessary spending.

Since the equilibrium business cycle is the result of changes in the technology behind the production of goods and services, and includes the assumption that prices are flexible and markets clear, there is no multiplier effect. Any increase in nominal spending would be transmitted to the price level, leaving real variables unaffected.

6. In the new Keynesian model, the increase in expected wealth will cause people to increase consumption and aggregate demand. In the sticky price model, businesses will respond to the increase in demand by increasing employment and output. The "prophecy" of increased wealth is self fulfilling. In the equilibrium business cycle model, there would be no increase in the productivity of labor or capital, so no change in the demand for resources. Current consumption would increase and savings would fall. Interest rates would be higher and the investment lower than it would otherwise be. (The higher interest rates may generate a positive effect on labor supply; although this would be limited by the income effect (people would feel wealthier so they would increase leisure.) Any increase in current GDP would be limited, and future output would be smaller due to the reduction in capital.

7. Sticky wages generate similar effects on GDP as sticky prices, but the impact on real wages differs in the two models. The sticky wage model predicts countercyclical real wages. Keynes might have been influenced by the persistently high unemployment rates of the Great Depression; after all, the sticky wage assumption, unlike the alternatives, does generate "involuntary" unemployment.

Chapter 17: World Markets in Goods and Credit

Chapter Summary:

The analysis so far has been conducted under the assumption of a closed economy. The final two chapters extend the model to include the flows of goods and assets across national borders. This chapter introduces basic concepts of **balance of payments** accounting, and proceeds to analyze the determinants of the **current account balance**. The major impact of opening the economy in this case is found in the international credit markets, where the differences between global real interest rates and domestic real interest rates induce changes in the flow of capital. When real national savings is less than net domestic investment, the difference must be financed by an inflow of capital from abroad. Because domestic real interest rates are procyclical, changes in the current account balance will be typically be countercyclical.

Of course, differences in the real interest rate are not the only determinant of current account balances. Temporary changes in national savings rates can have any number of other causes, war or political instability are two common examples. The twin deficits theory is also presented and it is shown that when Ricardian equivalence does not hold, government deficits will tend to increase the current account deficit. Empirical evidence on the twin deficits theory is examined in the "Back to Reality" section on page 433. The current account deficit can also be influenced by changes in the **terms of trade.** An increase in the price level of exports relative to imports generates effects similar to a technological improvement. Permanent improvements in the terms of trade are likely to produce relatively large increases in investment spending which will be associated with larger current account deficits. This analysis is supported by empirical evidence from the oil exporting countries.

Finally the chapter concludes with a discussion of the effects of globalization on the technology parameter A. The increase in the volume of trade leads to increases in A which cause higher rates of economic growth and per capita income.

Chapter Outline:

I. History of the U.S Current-Account Balance

II. Determinants of the Current-Account Balance
   a. Economic Fluctuations
   b. Harvest Failures, Government Purchases, Developing Countries
   c. Examples of International Borrowing and Lending

d. The Current-Account Deficit and Budget Deficit

III. The Terms of Trade

a. The Terms of Trade and the Current-Account Balance

a. The Terms of Trade and Investment

b. Empirical Evidence from Oil Producers

IV. The Volume Of International Trade

Teaching Tips:

1. I recall very little of what my professors said during my freshman year of college. But I recall vividly the day that my economics professor opined that the central bank policy of Japan had more influence over our trade deficit than any trade restrictions our government might adopt. Because that statement was so contrary to my preconceptions, it motivated me to learn more about the real causes and consequences of trade deficits. This chapter presents a real opportunity to challenge our students to think critically about globalization.

2. The previous chapter reviewed the various explanations for the Great Depression, but the current chapter adds another potential candidate: the collapse in the volume of trade that occurred during the period. The Smoot-Hawley tariffs of 1931 were part of a world wide increase in protectionist measures that lead to the unwinding of globalization. Using the arguments from the last section of the paper, we can see this could produce results similar to a negative technology shock.

3. A simple review of the principle of comparative advantage can help students understand how the volume of trade relates to productivity.

4. Is the U.S. suffering from an unhealthy addiction to foreign capital? Consider having students debate the topic in class. There are plenty of resources for them to refer to, including this one from BusinessWeek:
http://www.businessweek.com/magazine/content/05_28/b3942001_mz001.htm

5. This is a dense chapter which can be overwhelming to students who have encountered these kinds of concepts before. In this case, a simple diagram (shown below) may help to illustrate some of the major points. Using interest rates on the vertical axis and real GDP on the horizontal axis, and assuming, for simplicity, a vertical aggregate supply curve as a function of the interest rate, the

differences between the aggregate supply curve and aggregate demand curve can be interpreted as the current account balance. For example, consider using the diagram to illustrate the Barro's harvest failure example on page 430. In this case,
the AS shift the curve to the left, but consumption smoothing means that the aggregate demand curve will not shift as much. (see the second diagram below) The differential between domestic and world interest rates will increase, and the current account deficit will grow. Similarly, if Ricardian equivalence fails, an increase in the budget deficit will shift AD to the right with no corresponding increase in AS. Once again, the interest rate differential and the current account deficit will grow.

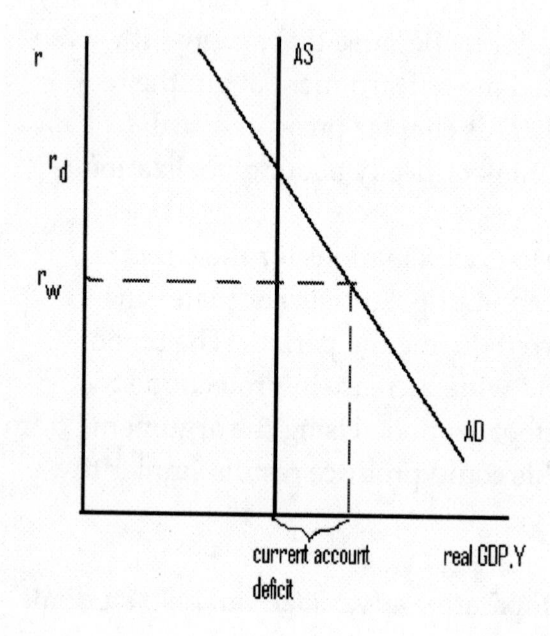

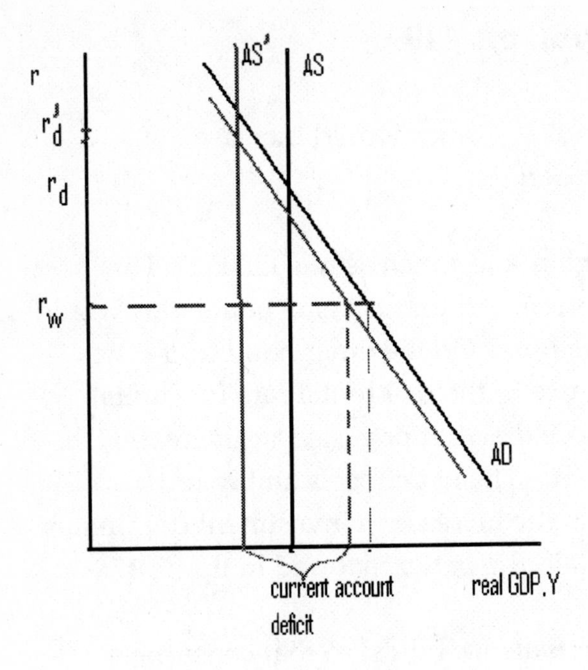

Answers to review questions, pg. 440

1. The current account in the balance of payments includes trade flows and net asset income. Every transaction which contributes to a deficit in one country (imports for example) would create the opposite effect in its partner's balance of payments (exports in this case). Another way to think of this is that for every current account deficit there is a capital account surplus; the nation would be a net importer of capital (a net borrower). It is impossible for every country to have a capital account surplus, because every loan must have both borrower and lender.

2. The current account deficit is the different between national savings and investment (see equation 17.11 on page 427). An increase in the budget deficit would reduce national savings if there were no Ricardian equivalence effects on private saving. In this case, the reduction in national savings would have the effect of increasing the current account deficit.

Answers to Problems for discussion, pg. 440

3. a. As discussed in chapter 9, the technology shock would increase employment, capital utilization and real GDP,Y.

b. Consumption will increase, although not as much as real GDP,Y. This means that net national savings will increase. All things being equal, this would move the current account balance into surplus. On the other hand domestic investment will also increase, due to the rise in the real rental rate for capital services. If domestic investment rises more than national savings increases, the current account will move toward a deficit. The net effect is ambiguous; however empirical evidence suggests that the increase in investment dominates the increase in saving, which would explain the patterns found in figure 17.6.

4. For all answers, assume Ricardian equivalence holds, so that consumers reduce private savings in response to the increase in government saving. We will assume that the tax revenue is used to reduce a budget deficit rather than an increase in government spending.

a. Because the change in wage rates is permanent, there is no intertemporal substitution effect on labor income. Any effects on labor supply will be relatively small, but negative. The reduction in labor employed will reduce the rate of return on capital ownership, resulting in lower rates of investment. As a result, the current account will move toward a surplus.

b. The effects here are similar to part (a) above, but magnified due to the intertemporal substitution effect. The current account will move toward a surplus while the tax is in effect, then move back to a deficit when the tax is removed.

c. The tax on asset income permanently reduces the after tax rate of return on capital ownership, reducing investment and moving the economy toward surplus.

d. The temporary tax on consumption leads to an increase in savings in the current period due to the intertemporal substitution effect. There may also be a reduction in labor supply because the after tax real wage rate has effectively been reduced. Both of these will tend to move the current account toward a surplus.

In future periods, these effects will be reversed as consumers attempt complete the intertemporal substitution.

5. In the case where the terms of trade improve due to foreign demand fo the exported good, the current account moves toward a surplus. However in this example, the country has experienced a crop failure which reduces real GDP,Y. Because this is seen as a temporary event, consumption smoothing will cause a reduction in saving and a move toward a current account deficit. The improvement in the terms of trade will work in the other direction, but probably not enough to move the current account to a surplus.

Chapter 18: Exchange Rates

Chapter Summary:

The open economy model is expanded to include different currencies. The concept of **purchasing power parity** for tradable goods is defined, as are the concepts of **nominal and real exchange rates**. The purchasing power parity condition is shown to be a powerful predictor of changes in real exchange rates over time, although it cannot explain short run variability in these rates. In the long run, differences in inflation rates are shown to be important causes of movements in nominal exchange rates, and differences in expected inflation rates are the major determinant of international differences in nominal interest rates. The concept of **interest rate parity** implies that differences in nominal interest rates must be offset by expected movements in nominal exchange rates.

Differences in the monetary policies of various countries may be expected to exert powerful influences on nominal exchange rates while leaving real exchange rates unchanged. On the other hand, countries which attempt to maintain a fixed nominal exchange rate must adapt their monetary policies to bring their nominal exchange rate target into alignment with the real exchange rate. Movements of international reserves in a **fixed exchange rate** system (such as the **Bretton Woods System)**, are supposed to automatically change the nominal quantity of money; the central bank must passively respond to changes in international reserves. In this case, the choice of inflation rate is largely determined by the monetary policy of one's trading partners. On the other hand, if central banks may choose to actively manage the money supply, in which case other policy options must be used to eliminate imbalances. These include **devaluation,** but trade barriers and foreign exchange controls may also be used. All of these options can have negative economic effects, so a country may wish to move to a **flexible exchange** rate if it wishes to maintain sovereignty over its domestic monetary policy. The chapter ends with a discussion of the relative strengths of the two exchange rate regimes. One of the key points in this section is that fixed exchange rates are preferred by countries seeking an external constraint on monetary policy. The experience of Argentina in 2001 demonstrates the hazards of this approach. It is also shown that price and wage stickiness, immobility of capital and labor, and structural differences in the economy make adjustments very difficult in a fixed exchange rate system.

Chapter Outline:

I. Different Currencies and Exchange Rates

II. Interest-Rate Parity

III. Fixed Exchange Rates

  A. Purchasing Power Parity Under Fixed Exchange Rates

  B. The Nominal Quantity of Money Under Fixed Exchange Rate

  C. Devaluation and Revaluation

IV. Flexible Exchange Rates : A Comparison

Teaching Tips:

1. The Economist magazine has a wealth of information on international reserves, nominal interest rates, nominal exchange rates, economic growth rates in the back pages of each issue. Students can apply the concepts of this chapter to identify the differentials in inflation rates and interest rates that exist, and make predictions about the future movement of nominal exchange rates.

2. The presentation in this chapter used equations rather than diagrams to illustrate the major concepts. As always, frequent use of simple numerical examples will make an abstract concept more concrete.

3. The last two chapters contain a lot of material and constitute a brief survey of international finance. Adequate time must be reserved toward the end of the course for covering these topics in depth.

4. Students may intuitively feel that a "strong dollar" is good for the economy. The theory presented in the chapter implies that the real exchange rate is determined by factors beyond the government's control. A "strong dollar" simply means a nominal exchange rate that can at best provide only temporary effects on the U.S. economy. Discuss with students what these policies are, and whether or not they are desirable for their own sake, regardless of their impact on nominal exchange rates.

Answers to review questions, pg. 465

1. The nominal exchange rate is the rate at which one currency can be traded for another in the foreign exchange market. The real exchange rate adjusts the nominal values for differences in the price level of the two nations. For example, if the price level is 1 in the domestic economy and 4 in the foreign economy, then a nominal exchange rate of 4:1 would generate a real exchange rate of $(4/4)/(1/1) = 1$. In this example the domestic currency can purchase 4 units of the foreign currency, but only 1 units of the foreign GDP. A fixed exchange rate is based on nominal values.

2. The condition is based on the theory that arbitrage (buying goods in markets where the price is low and selling them in markets where the price is high) will tend to eliminate differences in the price of goods in different markets. The equations are based on the assumption that all goods are tradable goods and the transportation costs are relatively insignificant. Another condition is that each country produces some of each good- if one country's exports a good for which there is no suitable substitute, then the terms of trade may favor that country and PPP will not hold.

3. Interest rate parity is based on the concept of arbitrage in asset markets. Assuming that the real exchange rate is one (PPP holds), then the differences in nominal interest rates between countries must be attributable differences in inflation rates. The rationale is that arbitrage will cause real interest rates available in each country to converge.

4. In a fixed exchange rate system, monetary policy must produce an inflation rate compatible with the targeted exchange rate. Increases in the supply of money will create inflation which would put downward pressure on the nominal exchange rate. For example consider a country with a targeted nominal exchange rate of 2. If the real exchange rate is equal to one, then the foreign price level must be twice the domestic price level: $P^f = \circledcirc P$ implies $P^f/P=2$. Inflation in the domestic economy must be equal to inflation in the foreign economy in order to maintain $\circledcirc=2$. In the short run, a central bank may attempt to block the tendency of real exchange rates to converge to one by intervening in the foreign exchange market, using foreign exchange reserves to create a kind of artificial demand for their currency. However, this would reduce the foreign exchange reserves of the central bank. Trade barriers and foreign exchange controls are

policy options which could be used to limit the demand for foreign exchange and reduce the need for central bank intervention.

5. The real exchange rate in the long run will tend to be equal to one, therefore, differences in the ratio of the price level in the two countries must be accommodated by movements in the nominal exchange rate. The main advantage of the flexible exchange rate system is that it permits Brazil to pursue its monetary policy unconstrained by nominal exchange rate targets. If Brazil pursued inflationary policies in a fixed exchange rate system, then the revaluation that would occur would have destabilizing effects on the economy, as it did for Argentina in 2001.

Answers to Problems for discussion, pg. 465-466

7. a. In order to maintain its exchange rate target, the central bank could increase the nominal money supply to accommodate the increased demand for money. The growth in the nominal money supply would maintain prices and exchange rates.

b. If no action is taken by the Chinese central bank, an increase in money demand would reduce the price level in China and cause the currency to appreciate.

8. Answers may vary, but in general, expect the data to confirm that the higher the inflation rate differential, the higher the growth rate in the nominal exchange rate.

9. a. The U.S. was facing a balance of payments deficit because the nominal rate overvalued the U.S. dollar. The foreign exchange and gold reserves of the U.S. were decreasing and the nation's leaders were unwilling to sacrifice domestic economic policies for the sake of maintaining the value of the dollar in foreign exchange markets.

b. Doubling the price of gold was one option; that would be a severe devaluation of the dollar and might have caused the same kinds of problems for the U.S. economy that East Asia experienced in 1997 and Argentina experienced in 2001. Other options included trade restrictions, a more restrictive monetary policy to reduce inflation and raise nominal interest rates. Under the classical theory of the gold standard, the reduction in gold reserves should have reduced the nominal money supply in the U.S., causing reductions in nominal prices which might have boosted exports and stopped the outflow of reserves. Traditionally, central banks would have encouraged these adjustments by raising nominal interest rates and slowing the growth in the nominal money supply. All of these "austerity" measures were unattractive to an administration that was reluctant to risk a slowing economy heading into an election year. Nixon ended up imposing wage and price controls on the economy that delayed the impact of the inflationary policies for a time; but inflation continued to rise when the price controls expired and the U.S. experienced high inflation rates throughout the 1970's. The moral of the story is that if you are going to live with a fixed exchange rate, you must be willing to adjust policies long before there is a crisis.

10. a. In this case the real exchange rate deviates from the nominal exchange rate. Perhaps the cost of shipping gold between London and New York can explain part of this deviation. If our New Yorker spends his $1000 on 200 ounces of gold and ships it to London, where he sells it for 200L. He then purchases $1200 with the proceeds, pays the shipping fees of $10 (1% of $1000 shipped). His profit is $190.

b. The Londoner can purchase 200 ounces of gold, ship it, and sell it in NY for $1000. The proceeds can be used to purchase 250L , 2 of which are used to pay the shipping fee, leaving her with a profit of 48L.

c. If the exchange rate falls outside of the gold points (4.95<1/◎<5.05 in our example) then it will be profitable to ship gold. In order to "repatriate" the profits, the seller of gold will seek to convert the proceeds into their own currency. Consider the example in part (b) above. The Londoner sells gold in New York, and then trades dollars for pounds, which would cause the pound to appreciate. In this case, the exchange rate would move from its initial level of $4/L per to $4.95/L.per pound. At that point it would no longer be profitable to ship the gold from London to New York.

11. When the bond is purchased, a futures contract for the same amount can be purchased at the same time. The euros earned when the bond matures can be used to satisfy the contract, and the holder will receive the $ equivalent based on today's exchange rates. Of course, there will be transactions costs associated with the purchase of the contract, but this is something like an insurance premium; the buyer is willing to pay a premium in order to reduce the risk of adverse movements in the exchange rate.